Nita Mehta's™

The Ultimate Beauty BOOK

Author: Nita Mehta
Edited by: Vaneeta Vaid

Nita Mehta's™

The Ultimate Beauty BOOK

SNAB Excellence in Books

Snab Publishers Pvt Ltd

Corporate Office
3A/3, Asaf Ali Road, New Delhi 110 002
Phone: +91 11 2325 2948, 2325 0091
Telefax: +91 11 2325 0091
E-mail: nitamehta@nitamehta.com
Website: www.nitamehta.com

Editorial and Marketing office
E-159, Greater Kailash II, New Delhi 110 048

Typesetting by National Information Technology Academy
3A/3, Asaf Ali Road, New Delhi 110 002

ISBN 978-81-7869-420-7

First Print 2014

Cover Designed by: SNAB Excellence in Books

Printed in India at Infinity Advertising Services (P) Ltd, New Delhi

Price: Rs. 250/-

Nita Mehta Books Distributors & Publishers

Distributed by :
NITA MEHTA BOOKS
3A/3, Asaf Ali Road, New Delhi - 02
Distribution Centre :
D16/1, Okhla Industrial Area, Phase-I,
New Delhi - 110020
Tel.: 26813199, 26813200
E-mail: nitamehta.mehta@gmail.com

Contributing Writers :
Anurag Mehta
Tanya Mehta
Subhash Mehta
Editor :
Vaneeta Vaid

Introduction

Our grandmothers and even our mothers took time to painstakingly draw resources from every day natural bounties to beautify themselves and us. Oiling, massaging, exfoliating, all collected to make a hearty statement that proclaimed, 'Here are the implements so you can preserve a beautiful you forever'. Years document the fact that they are very right. Along with external tools, which could be natural or even out of a bottle, all this was very much needed. Anyone asking for reasons would be told, "You may be born healthy and beautiful, but the pressures of modern lifestyles, weather, etc. can really do much damage. So protect your skin and mind with the knowledge of beauty care. A thought also intruded within these perceptions and of course later on verified by doctors that diet, exercise as well as everything else aided one to preserve beauty. The ultimate beauty book aims at covering all aspects of beauty. It is a unique collection of practical suggestions and recipes that works like a beauty encyclopaedia for any one looking for beauty care. Relying on the adage that the universal concept of beauty is radiant hair, skin, eyes, hands and feet as well as the inner confidence with the right attitude, we know our readers will love this book.

Nita Mehta

Contents

DRESS RIGHT 56

PERFUMED 60

BEAUTIFULLY PREGNANT 62

TOWARDS A FITTER YOU 70

RECIPES

Silken tresses, through which you can run your fingers easily is a wish every women has. Hair care has created it's own industry in modern times. During ancient times focus on beautiful, lustrous hair is portrayed by many temple sculptures that show women caring for their hair with different herbs and fruits! Even now herbs such as bhringaraj (Eclipta alba) which is known in Ayurveda as 'the king of the hair', and brahmi are used in hair products. Bhringaraj promotes hair growth, stops and reverses balding and premature greying and cools the head to keep the hair lustrous. Today in modern times, we have working ladies, busy ladiesthe list goes on... In this section we try and bring forth some hair care routines that are not too time consuming.

Hair Care

In India women, have always considered long, thick hair as a an asset! The older generation never failed to advice the younger generation about keeping hair long and healthy because they felt a head of shiny, well-maintained hair provides immediate beauty to any woman! In a tradition followed by their grandmothers and then their mothers, many working girls in the cities follow a special Sunday routine: they oil their hair well and plait it loosely, only to wash it the next morning. According to popular belief, this intensive nourishing treatment enhances the length and thickness of hair. Good hair is directly connected to good health as well as balanced environment. Bad eating, weather conditions and ruthless handling results in hair loss, premature greying, weak roots etc. Environment we cannot challenge much, but we can protect ourselves. Then how do we fix ourselves internally in order to remain healthy and prevent hair damage?

HAIR COMPOSITION

Understanding the composition of hair is important since when we are younger, I feel unthinkingly we damage are hair always believing in the fact that it will re-grow! We forget that the extended follicles are dead but within our hair shafts their is a living process going on that needs our attention and care.

The living parts of hair are hair follicle, hair root, root sheath, and sebaceous gland that are beneath the skin!

Each strand of hair is made up of the medulla, cortex, and cuticle. The innermost region, the medulla, is not always present and is an open, unstructured region. The highly structural and organized cortex, or middle layer of the hair, is the primary source of mechanical strength and water uptake. The cortex contains melanin, which colors the fiber based on the number, distribution and types of melanin granules.

Shape

The shape of the follicle determines the shape of the cortex, and the shape of the fiber is related to how straight or curly the hair is. Asian hair typically has a round fiber and is quite straight. Oval and irregularly shaped fibers are generally more wavy or even curly.

Cuticle

Much of the shine that makes healthy hair so attractive is due to the cuticle. The hair cuticle is also said to be water resistant.

The cuticle is the outer covering. Its complex structure slides as the hair swells and is covered with a single molecular layer of lipid that makes the hair repel water. The diameter of human hair varies from 17 to 180 micrometers (0.00067 to 0.0071 in). There are two million small, tubular glands and sweat glands that produce watery fluids that cool the body by evaporation. The glands at the opening of the hair produce a fatty secretion that lubricates the hair and prevents it from drying.

Growth

Hair growth begins inside the hair follicle. The only "living" portion of the hair is found in the follicle. The hair that is visible is the hair shaft, which exhibits no biochemical activity and is considered "dead".

Scalp

Scalp skin, just like any other skin on the body, must be kept healthy to ensure a healthy body and healthy hair production. If the scalp is not cleaned regularly, by the removal of dead skin cells, toxins released through the skin or external hazards (such as bacteria, viruses, and chemicals) may create a breeding ground for infection.

Sebaceous Glands

The sebaceous glands in human skin produce sebum, which is composed primarily of fatty acids. Sebum acts to protect hair and skin, and can inhibit the growth of microorganisms on the skin. Sebum contributes to the skin's slightly acidic natural pH somewhere between 5 and 6.8 on the pH spectrum. This oily substance gives hair moisture and shine as it travels naturally down the hair shaft, and serves as a protective substance preventing the hair from drying out or absorbing excessive amounts of external substances. Sebum is also distributed down the hair shaft "mechanically" by brushing and combing. When sebum is present in excess, the roots of the hair can appear oily, greasy, and darker than normal, and the hair may stick together.

SHINY & CLEAN HAIR

Distribution of natural oil on scalp to make hair shiny

One way to distribute the hair's natural oils through the hair is by brushing with a natural bristle brush. The natural bristles effectively move the oil from the scalp through to the hair's mid-lengths and ends, nourishing these parts of the hair. Brushing the scalp also stimulates the sebaceous gland, which in turn produces more sebum, which gives hair moisture and shine.

Brushing Your Hair 100 strokes a day is a myth!

Too much brushing is not good for oily hair because it stimulates oil glands that are already over active. So, do not brush too much if you have oily hair.

For dry hair, correct brushing is important. Sometimes dryness of the scalp is due to improper brushing. The brush bristles must be first pressed gently into the scalp, and then carried gently down to the hair tips. If the hair is brushed superficially, the oil glands become lazy because you are not exercising them sufficiently & your hair remains dry.

Washing Hair

Washing hair removes excess sweat and oil, as well as unwanted products from the hair and scalp. Often hair is washed as part of a shower or bathing with shampoo, a specialized surfactant. Shampoos work by applying water and shampoo to the hair. The shampoo breaks the surface tension of the water, allowing the hair to become soaked. This is known as the wetting action. The wetting action is caused by the head of the shampoo molecule attracting the water to the hair shaft. Conversely, the tail of the shampoo molecule is attracted to the grease, dirt and oil on the hair shaft. The physical action of shampooing makes the grease and dirt become an emulsion that is then rinsed away with the water. This is known as the emulsifying action.

If you opt for ready made shampoo...

Egg shampoos are good for DRY OR NORMAL hair.

For OILY HAIR, use a lemon based shampoo.

Herbal Shampoo

2 reethas (break to remove seeds), 2 shikakai pods, 2 tbsp dried amla

1. Mix all ingredients together with 2 cups of water in a pan at night. Boil in the morning till it is reduced to half.
2. Remove from fire and cool. Mash the herbs well.
3. Strain through a plastic soup strainer. Use this water as a shampoo on wet hair.

There will be no lather but the hair will certainly get cleaned.

Conditioning Hair

Henna as a conditioner for giving bounce & body to limp hair...

Mix henna powder with some lemon juice. Add enough curd to form a thin paste. Apply on the hair, dividing it into sections. Shampoo after ½ hour.

For giving a shine to the hair...

Give a final rinse to the hair after your head bath with juice of 1 lemon or a few drops of vinegar added to ¼ bucket of water.

Conditioning with bottled mixture is a way of moisturising your hair and preventing it from being coarse, dull and dry. This is done after shampooing hair. However some people do not need conditioners since they already have very moist scalps that lead to oily hair. It is important to wash off all conditioner when you rinse off.

Hair do's and dont's

Treat your hair gently and with care.

Never comb very wet hair.

Combing and brushing should be done when the scalp is at least partially dry.

Use a wide toothed comb on your hair first, when the hair is still wet.

Drying the hair calls for care.

Avoid electric driers. Just wrap your hair with a dry towel and let it absorb the water.

Don't scrub-dry as that would put tension at the hair roots, pulling out some hair and weakening others. Remember, the scalp's hold on hair is weaker when it is wet.

HAIR OIL MASSAGE

Oiling Hair

Oiling of scalp or champi is usually done before shampooing. Over the years are grand mothers have claimed that oil massages for the hair is important since it has a multi-dimensional effect. Oil forms a protective layers for the hair shaft. Correct massaging techniques increases or stimulates the circulation of blood to the scalp, helps to bring the nutrients and nourishes hair. It is also considered to be a great way to relax.

Scalp Massage

(i) First oil your hair with warm oil nicely.

(ii) Start your scalp massage at the hair - line at the nape of the head.

(iii) Grip the scalp firmly with fingertips of both hands and drawing the fingertips together and apart with a slow pinching movement as you push up towards the crown of the head. This brings the circulation to the scalp.

(iv) Repeat 2-3 times and then move the fingertips to the hairline above the front hairline and push backwards.

BENEFITS : This movement causes actual scalp friction and is excellent for permanent waved heads, falling hair that is inclined to come out easily.

Massage with Onion/Garlic Juice

Massage onion/garlic juice into the scalp to prevent hair loss and boost hair re-growth.

Benefits of Amla

(i) Drink a mixture of ground amla in water before you sleep. Vitamin C from this boosts hair health.

(ii) Soak amla, reetha and shikakai in water overnight, strain in the morning and apply to the scalp. Leave in for 30 minutes. Rinse well with water. This stimulates hair follicles and strengthens hair.

Home-made oil for hair

½ cup coconut oil, a few curry leaves - chopped

Method

(i) Heat oil in a heavy bottomed pan. Add chopped curry leaves to oil. Before getting the curry leaves too dark switch off the flame.

(ii) Apply to scalp with a gentle massage. Keep on for atleast on hour. Shampoo off.

Massage with Castor Oil

Apply several drops of castor oil to your scalp and massage it in thoroughly. Cover your hair with a shower cap, a scarf, or other covering and leave it on overnight. Shampoo and condition as usual the next morning. Alternately, mix a few drops of castor oil with olive oil or almond oil and follow the same directions.

Massage with Almond Oil

Take about a tablespoon of almond oil – more or less depending on the length and thickness of your hair – and massage it into your scalp, down to the ends of your hair. Leave it on for 15 minutes or so, then rinse your hair with cool water and shampoo as usual.

Correct Massaging Techniques

1. While massaging, place the fingers firmly on the head.
2. Work in small circular strokes, first clockwise and then anti-clockwise, moving the skin of the scalp as you do so. It is not your fingers but the skin of the scalp that should move.
3. By massaging this way, the blood circulation to the scalp is improved which keeps your hair strong and healthy.

HAIR MASKS

Egg and Olive Oil mask

Mix 2 egg yolks with 2 tablespoons of olive oil, then dilute the mixture with about half a cup of water. Slowly, thoroughly massage the resulting mask into your scalp. After letting it set for 15-20 minutes, shampoo.

Banana mask

Pick a soft, ripe banana, mask it up into a paste (use a food processor if you like, to make sure there aren't any chunks), apply it to your hair, and cover it with a plastic cap or bag. To lock in the nutrients, either wrap a hot towel around your head or remove the cap after 20 minutes and use your blow dryer long enough to help the banana set. Shampoo your hair and rinse well. Some users have reported difficulty rinsing out the banana, but if you end up with a smooth paste, rinsing should go smoothly. You can also add olive oil or almond oil to your paste, or a tablespoon of conditioner.

Whey Hair Rinse

Rich in proteins to lubricate and strengthen hair.

Whenever you make paneer at home, collect the whey (greenish liquid). Strain and store in a bottle. Rub in the scalp on wet hair. Rinse with fresh water.

For Dry, Lifeless Hair...

1. Rub a little warm olive oil or coconut oil right into the roots of the hair by dividing the hair into sections.
2. Soak a towel in steaming hot water and squeeze and wrap it around the scalp for 10-15 minutes. This opens up the pores of the scalp.
3. Give a second massage to the hair (without oil) for better and deeper absorption of oil.
4. Wash off after 1 hour.

For Dull, Lifeless Hair

1. Soak 1 tbsp methi dana (fenugreek seeds) in a little water. Grind to a paste.
2. Rub it into your scalp. Leave for ½ hour.
3. Shampoo the hair as usual.

COLOURING HAIR

Natural Hair Colouring

(i) Roast 2-3 tbsp of amla powder till black and add to henna (mehandi). Soak overnight. You will get a copperish colour on your hair due to the roasted amla powder.

(ii) For a rich copper colour, add a 1 tsp of eucalyptus (nilgiri) oil to henna (mehandi) before applying.

(iii) Boil the outer cover of a dark onion in a cup of water for a few minutes till it becomes half in quantity. Remove from fire and add 2 tsp of glycerine. Cool. Divide hair into sections and apply with cotton wool. Massage well. Wash your hair when dry to get a reddish tint on your hair.

Colouring Hair with Chemical dyes

If you have opted for dyeing your hair with the ready-made dyes (chemical dyes) available in the market, remember to apply a little cream on your eyebrows. This prevents the dye from coming in contact with the hair of the eye brows, while washing, forming a thin film on them.

Caution before Hair Colouring

When you get your hair coloured...

Some time back there was a disturbing news that a lady in UK had died from using hair dye. Though these allegations were never proved, it started an anxiety amongst many to verify if this would happen to them too! Sadly, allergies and the use of hair dyes are linked. Experts say that allergy to hair dyes is possible anytime. So a patch test is important every time one goes in for hair colouring! Chemicals in hair dyes play havoc! It is advised to be thoroughly sure of your hair dresser whilst colouring your hair.

Symptoms

(i) Local irritation on scalp

(ii) Major allergies that result in swelling and bloating.

(iii) Discoloration of forehead.

Safety Mantra : It is advised by experts that 'Undergo formal patch testing at an allergy (dermatology) clinic. The main chemicals that cause problems in hair-dyes are well known, and are available in patch-test form. Patch test a range of products yourself (unless you have suffered a severe reaction from hair dyes previously). Patch test by dabbing a small amount of the dye solution either behind the ear or on the inner elbow, leave to dry, and leave uncovered for 48hrs. If any irritation, rash or un-wellness occurs then do not use the product and wash it off your skin immediately.'

When choosing products, switch to non-permanent hair dyes. These generally use different, less troublesome chemicals. Henna is a very safe option. Other wise eat healthy to keep the tresses healthy and say no to colouring if you have any doubts of reactions!

Beware : Leaning your head back and getting a head wash after hair color, can also cause trouble. Hard nails, rough scrubbing and rubbing can cause hair damage and infections. Keeping your head at such an angle to be washed can also cause a nerve pinch.

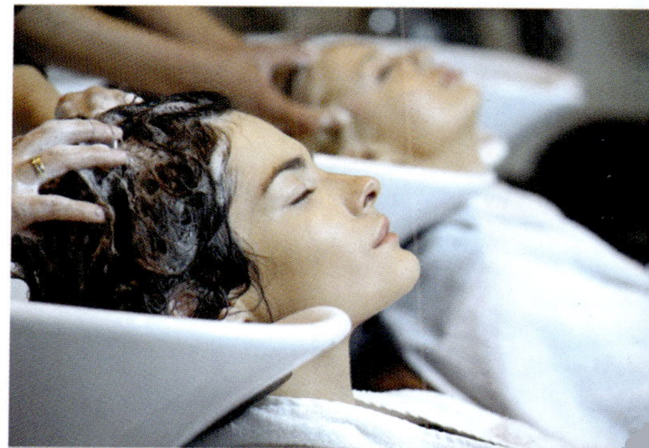

Safety Mantra : Make sure nobody uses your head as a rugby field! Instruct them to rub gently. Sit comfortably with the right posture to avoid a nerve pinch.

What is Highlighting Hair...

Foil highlighting is the process of using foil to separate strands of hair which will be lightened from strands of hair which will remain its natural color. The process is done by applying lightener to the hair that has been woven and separated using an applicator brush. The foil is then folded to protect the hair and surrounding area during the "processing" time. This is the amount of time required to achieve the desired results. In highlighting hair, hydrogen peroxide mixed with pigment is used to change the color of the strand.[2] This process is also used in applying "lowlights" to the hair. In this process, hair dyes are used to create strands of hair that are darker than the natural color.

Prevent Greying of Hair

To prevent early greying of hair, take 1 cup of strong black tea (without milk), and to this add 1 tbsp of salt. When cold, strain the tea and apply it on the roots with cotton wool. Leave it on for an hour, then wash it off. Do not shampoo it. I frequently use the left over tea in the teapot for my hair.

The cure or at least the slowing down of grey hair and falling off of hair can be effected by the use of amla. Regular massage of amla ground to paste and rubbed into the scalp has worked wonders in many cases, frequently reversing the process of greying or falling off of hair.

Every face shape has its typical hair style! It is always better to consult your hair stylist very conscientiously before any hair cut. Here a some suggestions for certain face shapes...

Hair Cuts for Face Shapes

For Round Faces: Long Layers, say experts

"If you want to wear a center part, the way to make it work for a round face is to have hair a few inches past your shoulders with layers that hit at the jaw," Prevent short layers from frizzing, which can add bulk around your face.

For Oval Faces: Blunt Bangs, say experts

"If your face tends to look long, cutting straight bangs across the brow line can break up the length by creating the illusion of width," hair dressers say.

For Square Faces: Wavy Ends

Try waves from the ears down, which helps obscure any severity in the jawline," Use a large round brush to smooth hair.

For Heart Faces: Bouncy Bob

Use a round brush and volumizing spray. Fill in the area around the jaw line and tone down the triangle look, for more emphasis.

HAIR OPTIONS...

Hair styling has added to its glamour quotient by introducing the option of hair extensions! The Hows and No's are discussed below...

The worst nightmare for anyone is to lose hair! Go bald??? No, no, never! Vanity has created many options to stall looking thin haired. Unfortunately, this self image of keeping a crowning glory at any cost can sometimes go very awry! Words like permanent hair weaves, hair extensions, etc, float enticingly around us. But be warned! It is only for people who have researched thoroughly and contacted a good technician who should go in for such fixes for the head! A large percentage of people suffer from male/female patterned hair loss, alopecia, trichotillomania, hormonal hair loss and those who have recently finished chemotherapy treatments. Getting a hair weave in these circumstances is not a bad idea. Not withstanding the fact that hair extensions or weaves are popular cosmetic hair enhancement tools!

What is a Hair Weave?

The hair weave we are writing here is usually referred to the attachment of artificial or human hair to make ones hair look fuller and long (sometimes). This is a completely non surgical method. People who experiment with such methods believe that they can alter their appearances almost at once! There are different kinds of hair extensions; some clip on, while others require weaving, gluing and wefting.

Some types of Extensions:

Clip-on: Most person prefer the clip-on type because they are easier to attach to your hair and you can take them off anytime. Plus they are better for your hair than having them glued or woven, which can make your hair weaker over time - this is because of the chemicals in the glue and because weaving pulls your real hair too tight.

The sew in method: This is to cornrow your hair. It involves the braiding of a person's natural hair. The braided hair is then sewn down and the hair weft extensions are sewn onto the braids.

Bonding: is the application of hair glue to a section of artificial hair then onto a person's natural hair; special hair adhesives are used in bonding to prevent damage to one's natural hair. This technique is commonly used and does not cause damage to the hair unless taken out without proper directions from a professional. It is advised that weave bonding be installed for up to 3 weeks because the glue begins to thin out.

The fusion method delivers one of the most versatile and most natural-looking weaves on the market. With this technique a machine similar to a hot glue gun is used to attach human hair extensions to individual strands of one's natural hair of about 1/8 to 1/4 inch squared sections for a truly authentic look. Another option for fusion attachments is using hair which is pre-tipped with a keratin adhesive. A heat clamp is then used to melt the adhesive to attach the extension hair to the natural hair. Fusion weave allows washing hair frequently and the use of regular hair products such as hair gels. Nonetheless this technique is very time consuming because it takes about 3 or more hours.

Netting: This is a technique which involves braiding natural tresses under a thin, breathable net that serves as a flat surface onto which stylists can weave extensions.

Lace fronts: The most recent development in weave extensions are lace fronts. Lace fronts are made from a nylon mesh material formed into a cap that is then hand-ventilated by knotting single strands of hair into the tiny openings of the cap, giving the hair a more natural and authentic continuity than typical extensions.

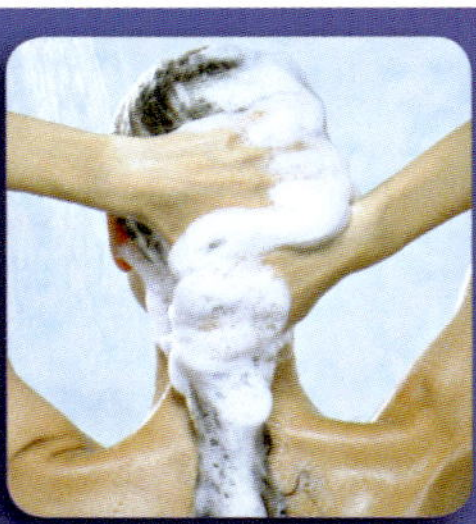

SHAMPOOING EXTENSIONS

Most human hair extensions can be treated as real hair, though you have to treat them more gently.

Shampooing of artificial hair integrations can be as easy as shampooing real hair, with some considerations. For instance, many manufacturers suggest using a mild shampoo, or even a wig shampoo.

Warning

- Do not invest in synthetic hair. The majority of these are flammable! Human hair is a better and safer investment.
- Hair weaving is not a permanent solution. Therefore, it is not a cure for baldness as weaving can never give you a natural-looking hairline.
- These side affects have been reported off and on by some using this method to have instant full head of hair. From blinding headaches, to patchy hair loss and sometimes permanent damage, doctors are now warning about the dangers of hair extensions.
- Don't leave your hair extensions in for too long. Your hair and scalp will need to be thoroughly cleansed after a few weeks.

SALOON TECHNIQUES AT HOME

Here are some hair-dresser's techniques which you can learn to use at home to create styles.

Blow Dry

You can make rolls with a brush without using rollers. After washing hair, dry them till slightly damp.

Divide hair into two halves. Divide each half into three sections. Take first section near the ear and roll in a brush. Put hot air through a dryer. Open the brush vertically (straight). Pin up this section. Take the next and then the third. Finally roll all three together and blow dry. Open, holding the brush vertically.

Similarly do the other side. Leave the hair to cool completely before you give it a final brush, or you will brush out the curls.

Give Bounce to Thin Hair

Never think of backcombing your hair to give it some body and bounce. Instead, after washing your hair, dry hair with a towel.

While still damp, bend and throw down the hair. Move your fingers in the hair or brush the hair from the roots to the tip. Take the hair on the left side to the right and vice versa. Now take the hair back with a gentle jerk and stand up as you do so. Repeat a few times and see the difference.

Finger-combing

Finger-combing works best on short wiry or curly hair and gives volume and shape.

Apply styling mousses all over, then use your fingers as you use a hairbrush, running your fingers through your hair in the direction your hairstyle should move. You can finger-comb using a blow-dryer or dry naturally.

Outward Curls

The hair should be damp (if you using Indian rollers). Take a section of hair according to the size of the roller. Place the roller at the bottom of that strand of hair, on the hair and roll up.

If the rollers are not firm, use bob pins to make them stick properly. Using a hair dryer, give hot air to each roller.

To open the rollers, remember to keep the rollers vertical (straight) while opening. If you open holding the roller horizontal as it is fitted, the curl will never come out properly. Leave the hair to cool completely before you give your hair a final brush.

Scrunching

Scrunching works on short or medium length hair which is slightly layered. It gives that tousled, soft look. To scrunch your hair whilst drying encourages lift at the roots. Grab your hair at the scalp in a fist, slightly open your fingers and blow warm air into the hair. Use styling mousse for a longer-lasting "scrunched" look.

EYES

The human eye is an organ that reacts to light and has several purposes. As a conscious sense organ, the mammalian eye allows vision. Rod and cone cells in the retina allow conscious light perception and vision including color differentiation and the perception of depth. The human eye can distinguish about 10 million colors. We tend to use our eyes all the time. Sometimes dull, tired and irritated eyes can mar a beautiful face. The following pages tell the reader how to prevent that and more...

Bright Eyes

(i) Get plenty of sleep. Aim for 7-8 hours sleep each night. Avoid late nights.

(ii) Treat sleep like a bank. Put in extra hours when you have overdrawn.

(iii) Dip cotton wool pads in ¼ cup chilled milk. Squeeze gently. Place on closed eyes for 10 minutes. Listen to soothing music.

(iv) Put cucumber slices on closed eyes for 10-15 minutes.

For Sparkling Eyes

(i) Soak 1 tsp of dried amla in a cup of clean water at night.

(ii) Next morning, strain the water through a muslin cloth. Dilute the water by adding another cup of water & splash the eyes with this water.

(iii) It may hurt the eyes slightly but it's certainly very good for eyes.

Puffy Eyes

Rub a slice of raw potato gently on the area around the eyes.

OR

Grate a potato & tie it in a muslin cloth. Keep on the eyes. This relieves puffiness and makes the eyes fresh and clear.

Dark Circles

Lack of sleep may be a cause for the dark circles under your eyes. Have enough sleep and a diet rich in fresh fruits and uncooked vegetables.

Apply juice of cucumber on the dark circles every day with a damp piece of cotton. To take out cucumber juice, grate a 1" piece of unpeeled cucumber and squeeze through a muslin cloth.

OR

Mix 1 tsp tomato pulp grated on the grater, a pinch of turmeric powder, ½ tsp lemon juice and 1 tsp gram flour together to form a paste. Apply with a brush on the dark circles every day. Wash off when it dries.

Itchy Eyes

To get some instant relief there are some easy to follow natural treatments for itchy eyes.

Rosewater

Rosewater is also a popular ingredient that can be used for minimizing the discomfort caused by itchiness in the eyes. Use rosewater to rinse your eyes at least twice a day. Apart from this you can also use rosewater as an eye drop. Put four to five drops of rose water into the inflamed eye and you will notice instant relief. Rosewater is one of the most effective home remedies for itchy eyes.

Fenugreek

Fenugreek can also bring instance relief from itching eyes. Take fenugreek seeds and soak them in water for seven to eight hours and then make a smooth paste out of it. Now apply the paste over your eyes and leave it for twenty minutes. Finally wash the paste off from your eyes with cold water. For better result, follow this home remedy twice daily.

Milk

Milk is also one of the popular home remedies to cure itchy eyes. Take cold milk and dab a cotton ball in it and use it to rub around the eyes. You can also place the cotton ball soaked in milk on the eyes to enjoy an instant cooling effect. Follow this home remedy twice a day once in the morning and once in the evening.

Green Tea Bags

Green tea bags are healthy and can also be used to get relief from itchy eyes. To make an eye wash boil two green tea bags in one cup of distilled water and then allow the solution to cool completely. Use this solution to flush the eyes twice a day unless the problem of itchy eyes is solved completely.

MASSAGE AROUND THE EYES

(i) Do not stretch or rub the delicate skin around the eyes when applying any cream or lotion on your face. Any massage around the eyes should be done with a very light & a feathery touch.

(ii) Avoid the area around the eyes when you apply face masks as the skin around the eyes is very delicate.

(iii) Always massage with a light, feathery touch.

(iv) While massaging the skin around the eyes, start from the outer corner of your eye, move below your eye using your fore finger. As you reach near your nose, take a 'U' turn and massage with an extremely light touch over the upper lid towards the outer corner of the eye or the starting point.

(v) Massage both the eyes with fingers of both the hands simultaneously.

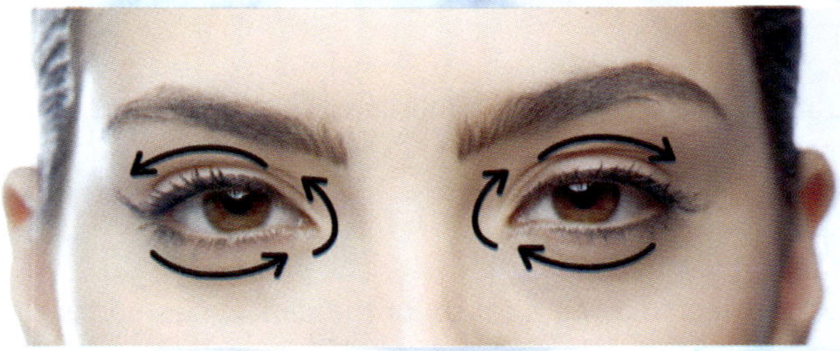

MAKE UP FOR DIFFERENT EYE SHAPES

Close Set Eyes

Apply eye shadow to the upper eyelids, blending the shadow upwards and outwards towards the outer corner of the eyes. Continue to blend until the shadow is considerably fainter in the area of the nose and the eye and somewhat darker at the outer corner. Line the eyes, leaving the inner corners of the eyes. Increase the distance between the eyebrows by removing hair in-between to make them appear wider apart.

Deep Set Eyes

Use a lighter shade of foundation immediately above the socket area of the upper eyelids and blend well. Do not use eyeshadow as the sunken effect will increase instead of decreasing.

Drooping Eyes

They can be given a lift by tilting the eyeliner upwards and outwards before it reaches the outer corner of the upper lid. The shadow should be winged upwards avoiding the area at the outer corner of the eyes.

Small Eyes

They can look larger by using two shades of shadow. Use a light shade on the upper eye lid and a darker shade on the crease. Apply the lower eye liner and kajal from the middle to the outside of the eye.

ORDER OF EYE MAKE UP

(a) Eye shadow
(b) Eye Liner (Kohl pencil or liquid eyeliner)
(c) Kajal
(d) Mascara

Eye Shadow : The shadow is applied only on the upper eyelid, leaving the space beneath the brows. If you wish, you may apply some shadow on the lower lash line to add colour.

Close your eye while applying the shadow. Start from the centre of the eye lid near the lashes and go upwards till the crease of the lid, leaving the space beneath the brows.

Apply some eye shadow with a thin brush, lightly beneath the eyes, next to the lower lash line, starting from the middle to the outer corner of the eye.

Eye Liners : The correct way to use an eye liner is outside the eye, just along the lash line with absolutely no gap. Line the upper lash line by running the pencil over the upper lashes leaving the inside corner of the eyes. In the same way run the pencil over the lower lashes, keeping the length which suits you. Lower your eyelids to see that no space (skin) shows below the line.

The soft, smudged look also looks good on some people.

Applying Liners : To apply the liner, always start from the middle of the eye to the outer corner and then starting at the inner corner, draw a line to join the line in the middle.

Kajal : Open your eyes and apply the kajal inside the eye, next to the lower lash line. You may wear your kajal along the full length of the eye or even keep it shorter - ¾, ½ or ¼ of the eye.
TiP : To make small eyes look bigger put only ½ length - starting from middle to the outer corner of the eye.

Mascara : Before applying mascara, remove all excess mascara on the brush by rubbing it on the sides of the bottle. There is a definite technique to applying mascara. First apply it on the top side of the upper lashes, stroking the colour down. Then on the underside of the top lashes, stroking the colour up. Avoid using the wand on the lower lashes for daytime; do so only for an 'event' evening. Apply two coats. Let the first coat dry completely; then apply the second coat, for two thin coats look more natural than one thick coat.

Coloured Mascara : If you are bold enough, try putting on a blue or brown mascara on your lashes after applying a coat of black mascara, for a stunning look.

Tip to Remove Mascara : Mascara must be removed very carefully to avoid damaging the delicate skin around the eyes. Try removing the final traces of mascara with a cotton bud dipped in cleanser.

Get It Right...

The Right Length of your Eyebrows

Right Start

Look straight in the mirror. To see where brows should start, hold a pencil vertically against one nostril. Where the pencil meets your brow is a good starting point. Repeat on the other side.

Right Endings

Hold a pencil vertically against one nostril. Angle it so that it aligns with the outer corner of the eye - where the pencil hits the brow is where the brow should end.

Scanty Eyebrows

(i) Make your eyebrows thick and shiny by applying castor oil on them.

(ii) Whenever you oil your hair, remember to rub oil on the eyebrows also.

Eye Care

Here are some quick eyes relaxation exercises.

- Eye rotation : Slowly rotate your eyes, first towards the right, five times. Rest at the slow count of five. Rotate to the left five times. Make sure you do a full circle slowly. This strengthens your eye muscles.
- After prolonged watching of Television and use of computer remember to blink your eyes. This is a very good exercise to protect vision.
- If you feel a strain in the eyes, cup your palms over your eyes and sit for at least for five minutes. This helps in relaxing your eye muscles.
- Sunning : For five minutes close your eyes and face the sun, (early morning sun), Sunbathe your eyes. Move slowly to one side to the other, feel the sun on your eyes. This improves blood circulation in the eyes.

Rubbing Eyes

Most people's eye pressure returns to normal when they stop rubbing and the temporary blip does no obvious long-term damage.

However, for people with certain eye conditions, an increase in eye pressure caused by hard, frequent or prolonged rubbing could be more serious.

For instance, people with progressive myopia – a common type of short-sightedness caused by a lengthened eyeball – can find their eyesight worsens. In some cases, their retina detaches from the back of the eye. Also bad quality make products cause the urge to rub. Be warned that the temporary relief you get is temporary - period. A serious permanent damage is definitely in the offing.

SKIN CARE

Skin - the largest organ in human body

The skin supports its own ecosystems of microorganisms, including yeasts and bacteria, which cannot be removed by any amount of cleaning. Oily surfaces, such as the face, may contain over 500 million bacteria per square inch. Despite these vast quantities, all of the bacteria found on the skin's surface would fit into a volume the size of a pea. In general, the microorganisms keep one another in check and are part of a healthy skin.

Cosmetics should be used carefully on the skin because these may cause allergic reactions. Each season requires suitable clothing in order to facilitate the evaporation of the sweat. Sunlight, water and air play an important role in keeping the skin healthy.

Fresh, healthy skin needs a lot of care. In these pages read the A to Z about your skin maintenance, specially your face.

Know Your Skin

It is always easier to look after your skin if you are sure about the type of skin you have.

Normal : The skin is smooth, finely textured, soft and supple.

Dry : The skin is usually thin and delicate, often flaky, and prone to fine lines.

Oily : The skin is shiny & coarsely textured, often with enlarged pores & prone to blackheads & spots.

Combination : This skin consists of both dry and oily areas. The fore head, nose & the chin are oily forming a 'T' shape of oily area on the face. The cheeks & temples (just above the end of the eye brows) are dry.

Daily Skin Care

Cleansing, toning, moisturising are the fundamental routine which should be followed for a glowing complexion. You may do it at night before going to bed. If you have an oily skin you should follow this routine in the morning too.

Cleansing : Wash your face with a good face wash. Do not wipe by rubbing the skin. Simply pat dry. For thorough cleansing, dip a piece of cotton wool in 1 tbsp milk. The milk should be unboiled preferably. Squeeze it gently. Rub on the face and neck in a circular, upward motion to deep cleanse your skin. This opens the pores of the skin and cleanses it thoroughly. Cleansing should continue until there are no traces of dirt on the cotton wool.

Toning : As cleansing opens pores, it is important to use an astringent to close them. An astringent also freshens your face besides closing the pores. Instead of a ready-made astringent, just splash chilled water on your face & then pat dry with a towel. Chilled water or preferably cold mineral water is an excellent astringent & skin freshener which tones your face well. Toning also removes the last traces of dirt.

Moisturizing : A moisturiser will replace natural oils lost through cleansing and toning, keeping your skin supple and protecting it against moisture loss. Use a herbal moisturizing lotion or a night cream. Lightly massage onto the skin using circular up & outward movements.

Massage the Right Way....

(i) Start at the collar bone and brush fingers up neck and under chin. Roll knuckles over cheeks and gently roll skin between fingers until it tingles. See sketch 1.

(ii) Position thumbs under chin and starting at the inner corners of eyes run fourth finger gently over brow bone and down below eyes into corners again. Massage with a very light touch. Sketch 2.

(iii) Place first and second fingers on temples and rotate firmly, without moving fingers, pressing as you go. Finish with a firm stroke towards the centre of the fore head. Massage the forehead upwards with the fingers of both the hands alternately. Sketch 3.

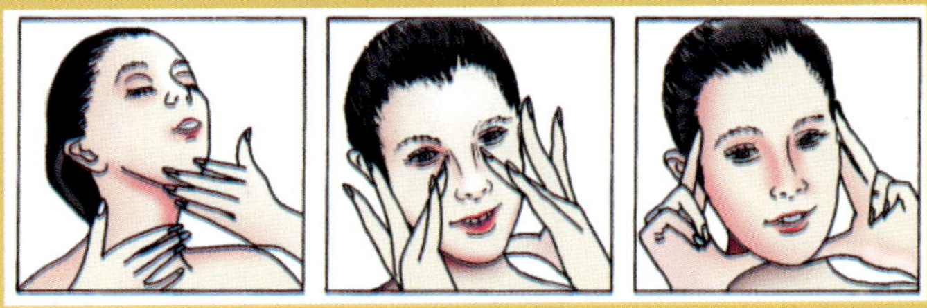

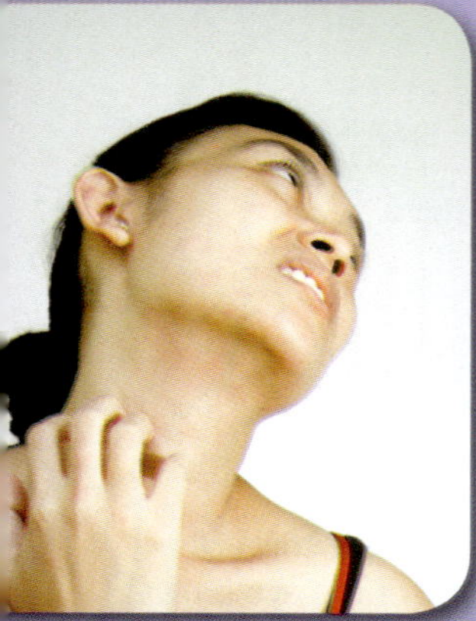

FACE SOLUTIONS

(i) Never forget the neck in all the face treatments, as it shows the same telltale signs as the face.

(ii) Apply the pastes and juices on an absolutely clean skin with a face brush.

(iii) Do not talk when you have applied some thing on your face.

(iv) For normal or dry skins, use milk or curd to make your pastes. Avoid lemon juice as it tends to dry the skin further. For oily skins, lemon juice is good.

Clear Pimples

(i) Wash and grind a few fresh mint leaves to a smooth paste. Apply and leave for ½ hour or apply every night before going to sleep. This helps in getting rid of pimples along with the blemishes.

(ii) Rub scrapped bitter gourd (karela) peels over the face to keep black heads and pimples away.

(iii) To remove marks left by pimples, mix 1 tsp radish (mooli) juice with 1 tsp buttermilk (lassi). Apply to the face with a face brush and wash off after 1 hour.

Clear Blemishes and Scars from Face

- Clean face with cotton wool dipped in rose water 1-2 times a day. It clears up and brightens the face.
- Blanch (soak and peel) a few almonds. Grind to a fine paste with 2 tbsp milk and 1 tbsp each of orange juice and carrot juice. Apply with a face brush on the face and neck. Leave for ½ hour, then wash off.
- Take the pulp of a ripe tomato. Add a few drops of lemon juice. Rub on the face and neck. Leave for 20-25 minutes. Wash off.
- If your skin is dry, rub a stick of sandalwood in milk and if your skin is oily, rub it in rose water and then apply on face. Leave for 1 hour and then wash with cold water.

Smooth and Soft Skin

- Grind 1 tsp chironji to a paste. Mix 1 tsp each of milk and curd. Apply and leave for 20 minutes before washing off.
- To 1 tsp of carrot juice, (grate some carrot and squeeze to get juice) add 1 tsp honey. Apply and remove after 15-20 minutes.
- Apply little grape juice on face and neck. Leave for 15-20 minutes before washing it off.
- Dip a cotton wool in some un-boiled milk. Pat all over face and neck. Leave for ½ hour and wash off. Lighten and Brighten Your Complexion
- Grind a few almonds in milk and apply on the face at bedtime. Keep it on for ½-1 hour and wash off.
- Soak chana dal (split gram) in milk overnight. Next morning grind to a paste. Mix a pinch of turmeric powder and a few drops of lemon juice. Apply and keep for ½ an hour before washing it off.

- Mix 1 tbsp milk, 1 tsp each of carrot juice, orange juice and honey. Apply, leave for 15-20 minutes and wash.
- Grate a small potato along with the peel. Squeeze to take out juice and apply the juice with a face brush on your face. Leave for 20 minutes till dry and then wash off.
- Mix 1 tbsp kheera (cucumber) juice, a few drops of lemon juice and a pinch of haldi (turmeric powder). Apply and keep for 25-30 minutes before washing.

Removing Dark Circles Around Eyes

- Apply kheera (cucumber) juice or potato juice around the eyes with a brush or cotton wool. You will find a change in 2-3 weeks. Simply grate a small potato or a 1" piece of kheera along with the peel and then squeeze within your palm to get juice. When you buy potatoes for the week, buy 7-8 small sized ones, keeping them aside and using one each day for your under eyes. Apply the juice not only under your eyes but on the complete face and neck since potatoes have a bleaching quality, keeping the face clear of blemishes.
- Take 1 tsp tomato juice, ½ tsp lemon juice, a pinch of haldi (turmeric powder) and ½ tsp besan (gram flour). Make a paste and apply. Leave for 10 minutes and wash off.

Remove Sunburn/Suntan

- Mix 1 tbsp tomato juice (grate tomato and squeeze through a muslin cloth to get juice) and 2 tbsp thick curd. Apply with a face brush. Wash after ½ hour.
- Mix 1 tsp olive oil with 1 tsp of vinegar and apply an hour before your bath.

Shrink Open Pores

- Mix 1 tbsp tomato juice and a few drops of lemon juice. Apply on open pores. Wash after 15-20 minutes.
- Rub ice everyday at the area where open pores are present. Wash face with cold water. Never use hot water on face.

Be Warned

Facials

Facials, polishes, massages can go very wrong if you land up at the wrong parlour! Some times products used by some parlours are cheap fakes. Unwittingly, you allow them to use it on your skin. Rashes, allergies, black spots etc. erupt and cause chaos to your health. Some times even permanent damage.

Safety Mantra : Make sure products used on your skin are of good quality and from reputed sources.

HANDLING MIDDLE AGE SKIN CRISIS

Dark Spots On the Cheeks

On reaching middle age, a lot of women develop dark spots on their cheeks and nose. The most effective treatment for this is to apply with a brush, a mixture of ½ tsp multani mitti mixed with 1 tsp radish (mooli) juice (grate 1½" piece of radish and squeeze within your hands to get the juice).

NOTE: When applying the mixture, keep away from the eyes and do not apply too close to the eyes. This mixture gives a burning sensation in the eyes and on the face at the beginning, but the skin gets used to it after a few days. It may also make the skin a little reddish which soon becomes all right.

Wrinkle Free Skin

By using the tips given below, you can prevent wrinkles to make your skin younger looking & wrinkle free.

- Mix 1 tbsp carrot juice with 1 tsp milk. Apply on your face and neck. It removes ugly age lines
- Take 1 tbsp egg white and 1 tsp rose water. Add 2 drops of glycerine. Mix well and apply on face and neck with a brush. Sit still for 20 minutes. Do not talk till mask is dry and hard. Rinse well.
- Mix 1 tsp olive oil and 1 tbsp egg white. Apply on face and neck and let it dry. Do not talk when this pack is on the face. Then remove it with a piece of cotton wool dipped in ½ cup hot water to which a pinch of mitha soda (soda bicarbonate) has been added.
- Take ½ tbsp cold malai (milk topping), add 4-5 drops lemon juice. Massage your face with this. Keep for 20-25 minutes and then wash off. **NOT RECOMMENDED FOR VERY OILY SKINS.**
- Apply papaya pulp (finely grate and mash a little ripe papaya) on the face and neck. Leave for ½ hour. Along with wrinkles your blemishes will also disappear. If you find the pulp messy, eat the papaya and rub the peel which has some papaya on it, on your face and neck.

Removing Stubborn Wrinkles

- Mix 1 tbsp honey and ½ tbsp carrot juice. To extract juice, grate a little carrot and squeeze it to get some juice. Apply on the face and neck. Leave for 20 minutes. Soak cotton wool in warm water to which a pinch of soda bicarb (mitha soda) has been added. Remove mask with it.

Preventing Wrinkles

- Massage your face & neck with almond oil (Badaam rogan) with upward, circular motion.
- Cut a vitamin E capsule open. Mix Vitamin E capsule (opened up) and enough glycerine to make a paste. Apply on your face with a brush in the upward direction. Wash off after 10-15 minutes.
- Fresh malai (not for oily skins) left on the face overnight, is very effective for wrinkles.
- An effective, simple exercise to keep your facial muscles tight. Fill your mouth with air as if you are filling air into a balloon. Keeping the air trapped in the mouth, carry it to the side into the cheek, thus blowing your cheek. Now rotate the air to the other cheek. Repeat it several times. You can feel the muscles being pulled. Do it any time - reading a book, driving a car...

BAN BLACKHEADS

Black-heads are caused by over active oil producing glands (sebaceous glands) of the skin. The excess secretion of oil expands and thickens the pores of the skin. The oil collects in the pores and hardens into a plug. The pores are then clogged with hardened sebum or oil. Since the pores are open, the tip of the clogged grease is exposed to the air and oxidizes, turning black. Hence, the name blackheads.

Washing the face twice a day with a medicated soap and lukewarm water helps reduce the oiliness of the skin surface and eliminates the chances of blackheads.

For Removing Blackheads...

1. Mix in a large pan 5-6 cups water, juice of 1 lemon
2. Keep the pan on fire to boil.
3. Rub cold cream on the blackheads.
4. Keep a large towel ready.
5. Remove the pan of boiling water from fire.
6. Bend over the steaming hot water and cover your head with the towel.
7. Steam for 10 minutes.
8. Rub the blackheads vigorously with a face towel.
9. Wash with chilled water. Repeat twice a week.

Grandmother's Tips for Blackheads

To avoid blackheads... Mix

1 tbsp husk obtained by sifting wheat flour (chokkar)

1 tsp milk (enough to form a thick, dry paste)

- Sift chakki ka atta of ordinary quality to get the husk. Make a very thick paste with milk & rub it on the blackheads on your nose for 1-2 minutes daily. You may rub the leftover on your face too.

For removing blackheads...

- Mix 1 tsp soda bi-carb (mitha soda) in 2-3 drops water to make a thick paste. Rub on your nose on the blackheads.

A GLOWING FACE

Beauty secrets for the week

NOTE: Remember to clean your face first before any beauty routine.

Monday

Scrub a piece of cucumber on your face & neck. Wash off with cold water after 15 minutes.

Tuesday

Rub half a tomato on your face & neck. Rinse off after 15-20 minutes.

Wednesday

Scrub a piece of lemon. Rinse off after 15-20 minutes. Rub in an upward and circular motion.

Repeat for the next three days of the week.

Sunday Routine

Mix

1 tbsp gram flour (besan), juice of ½ lemon
¼ tsp turmeric (haldi) powder, 2-3 tsp milk (unboiled)

1. Apply the paste on your face and neck with a face brush moving the brush upwards. Leave to dry. Rinse with cold water.
2. In winters you may add fresh malai (topping of milk) since besan makes your skin dry. If you have a dry skin, substitute malai for milk always.

FACE WORKOUT...

Remove Wrinkles form your Forehead

1. Raise your eyebrows towards your hairline.
2. Widen your eyes. Make them wider with each count. Relax. Repeat once again.

Get Rid of that Double Chin

1. Move head back in a tilt.
2. Place your lower lip over your upper lip.
3. Curl your tongue inward and press it against the roof of your mouth.
4. Now try and smile.

Face Tightening

1. Wash your hands or wear gloves.
2. Place entire length of thumbs inside both sides of your mouth between the teeth & lower lip.
3. Suck upper lip back into the teeth so that the thumbs are squeezed.

Remove Wrinkles from your Cheeks

1. Keep your head straight.
2. Blow air into your cheeks, keeping your mouth pursed.
3. Shift this air from one cheek to the other, to the count of 5 for each cheek. Relax, repeat once more.

SPECIAL MASKS FOR DIFFERENT SKINS

Understand your type of skin by reading on page 10 and unmask your beauty by deciding on the right face mask. Apply the mask atleast once a week with a flat face brush, moving the brush in the upward direction. A face mask helps to draw out dirt from clogged pores. It gives a smooth complexion to the user.

Potato Yoghurt Mask for Dry Skin

1. Wash and cut a small potato. Grate finely. Press the grated potato to extract the juice. Mix curd.
2. Apply on face and neck with a brush. Move the brush in the upward direction. Leave for 15 minutes. Wash off.

Multani Mitti with Rose Water for Oily Skin

1. Mix 1 tbsp multani mitti (fuller's earth) with enough rose water to make a paste. Apply the paste on the face and neck. Rinse off after 10-15 minutes.

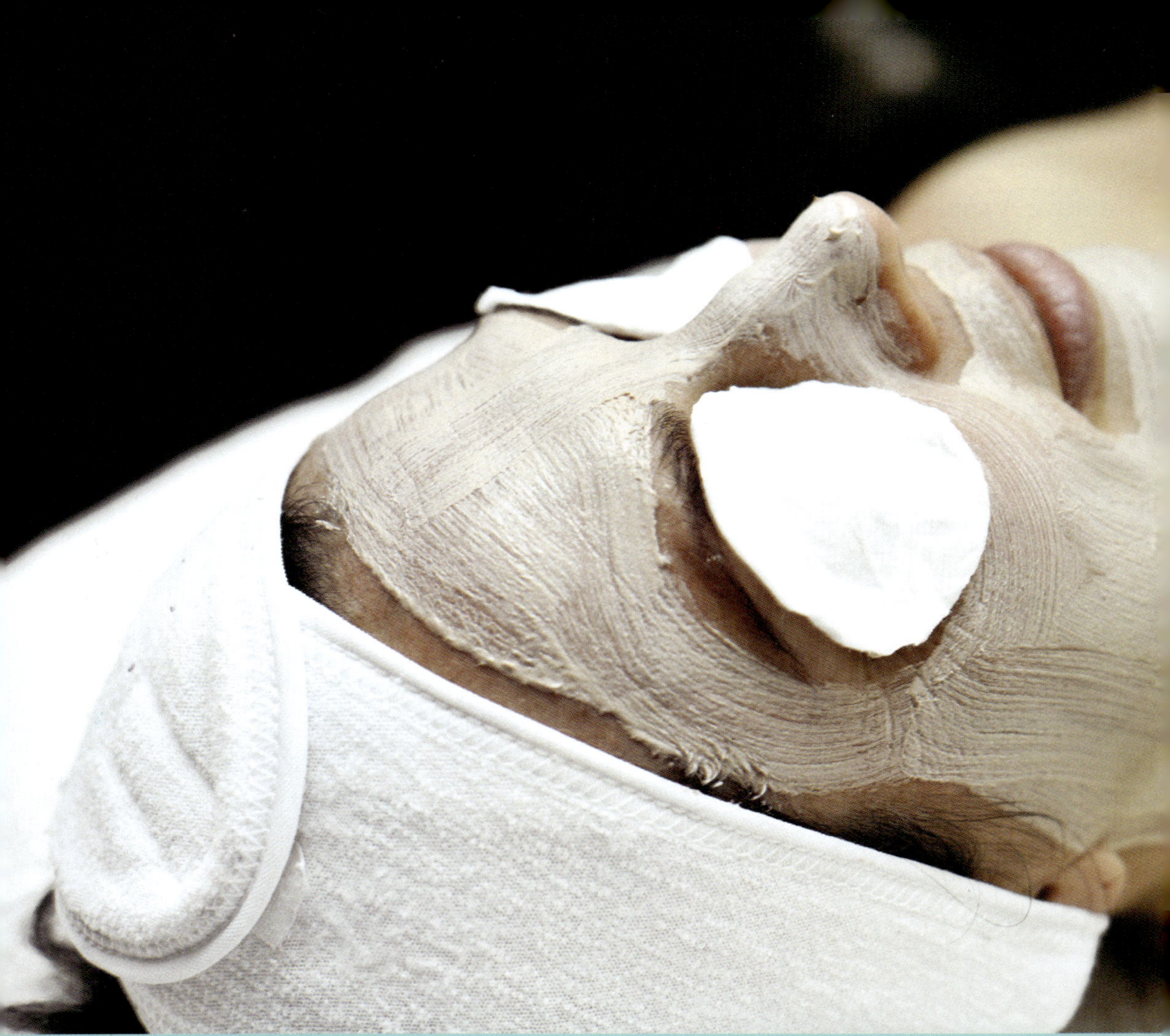

BEAUTY FROM YOUR KITCHEN

Its always good to know that you are applying the purest of pure stuff on your face! Keeping this in mind, here are some single ingredients, from your kitchen that can be used to make refreshing face applications...

Apple Vinegar

Mix 1 tsp olive oil with 1 tsp of apple vinegar and apply an hour before your bath on your face. Rinse off well. This gets rid of sun tan.

Mayonnaise

Wash your face. Take a spoonful of mayonnaise (preferably egg-less). Gently apply. Keep it on for 20 minutes. Let it dry; then wipe it off and rinse with tepid water.

Yogurt

Revitalise your skin by dabbing small scoops of yogurt on to the palms of your hands and gently rub it all over your face. Keep for 20 minutes. Wipe off with soft damp cloth. Wash off with tepid water.

Tomato

Mix 1 tbsp tomato juice and a few drops of lemon juice. Apply on open pores. Wash after 15-20 minutes.

Eggs

Take 1 tbsp egg white and 1 tsp rose water. Add 2 drops of glycerine. Mix well and apply on face and neck with a brush. Sit still for 20 minutes. Do not talk till mask is dry and hard. Rinse well.

Papaya

Apply papaya pulp (finely grate and mash a little ripe papaya) on the face and neck. Leave for ½ hour. Along with wrinkles your blemishes will also disappear. If you find the pulp messy, eat the papaya and rub the peel which has some papaya on it, on your face and neck. Wash off after 15 minutes.

Note: After applying some of these applications, please RELAX! Frowning or talking with the mask on can create fine wrinkles on your face.

MASSAGE

Good massage and diet are two recommended must do's for a glowing, relaxed skin care routine.

Self-massage

Most people who instinctively rub their neck or shoulders when their muscles are sore or tense have no idea that they are using this massage technique. Besides alleviating aches and pains, this is an excellent way for those in good health to use self-massage on a routine basis to prevent disease.

Loofah - dried fibrous residue of the cucumber relative Luffa cylindrical, can be used in the bath or shower to do self-massage, to improve dead skin and also to improve the blood circulation and drainage of the lymphatic system.

Self-massage is a proven remedy for fatigue, insomnia, muscle tension, muscle weakness, joint pain, circulatory disorders and skin problems. It may also help heal an injury, such as a sprain, by bringing fresh oxygen to the affected tissues.

Rubbing

To stimulate circulation and release muscle tension, rub your muscles in circular motions with your hands and fingers. Begin each massage by gently stroking the skin. Then, either using one hand or both hands, start rubbing your muscles. While using both hands, move them together or alternate between them. Work the strokes toward the heart.

I rub my painful, slightly stiff knees very gently for at least 100 circular motions with my palms and fingers, both clockwise and anti-clock wise in the morning. This relaxes the knee muscles which results in removing the stiffness and thus the pain.

Kneading

Using a little warm natural vegetable oil like olive oil or mustard oil, as a lubricant, work on your muscles as if you are kneading the bread dough.

I knead the painful parts of my knees for 10 minutes.

Vibrating

Use rhythmic knocking or lightly patting with your flat hands, to improve blood circulation and relax muscles. Finally, end every massage with gentle strokes, slowly moving outward.

Special masseurs also give a good body massage. But remember to appoint a trained masseur to do the job. Firm massage strokes warm the skin and assist the penetration of oil, takes at least 10 minutes. The massage can be done well over an hour.

Benefits of Massage

* Helps in healing of illness.
* Soothes pain.
* Removes anxiety.
* Benefits arthritis.
* Relief to hypertension.
* Migraine.
* Chronic fatigue.
* Improves blood circulation.
* Increases stimulation of lymphatic system, particularly lactic acid.
* Helps remove toxins that have built up in the muscles causing the stiffness and pain.
* Lactic acid is also built up after strong exercise, for this the athletes as well as tense office workers need massage.
* Massage helps human bonding, improves self esteem and we recognize the healing touch of the hands.

Massage Therapy Used in Home-remedies

Plant oils such as almond, apricot kernel and wheat germ have vitamins, which can be absorbed by the skin. Sweet almond oil contains vitamins F & E which assist nail growth, skin repair and is good for hands. Apricot kennel oil contains Vitamin A, which softens hardened skin on the feet. Wheat germ oil contains vitamin B. Lotions that contain cooling peppermint oil are also good for tired, aching feet.

Precautions:

1. Massage one body area at a time. Look carefully at your skin before beginning the massage.
2. In areas where the skin is red or painful, massage outward, being careful not to apply too much pressure. Pale areas should be stimulated with energetic massage.

HAIRLESS

Somewhere in the distant past it was considered uncouth for women to have hair on their body. This thought stayed. Today there are many ways to ensure smooth and hairless skin through various methods.

Shaving

This is removing hair with the help of a razor.

Do's & Dont's

1. Always buy a ladies razor.
2. Clean razor after use. Make sure you change the blade frequently.
3. A gentle scrub with a pumice stone can ensure no in-grown hair, which is a common problem whilst shaving.
4. Never dry shave. Lather up with soap and water first.
5. Never forget to soak the razor in anti-septic liquid before use.

Be warned : It is suspected that shaving regularly creates thick re-growth.

Waxing

This is removal of hair with wax.

Do's & Dont's

1. Wear loose clothing when getting a brazilian, bikini or leg waxing service done.
2. Allow your hair to grow out at least ¼ inch.
3. Never shave between waxing appointments. This distorts the hair growth cycle.
4. Wear cotton or no underwear at night to allow the area to breathe.
5. Avoid having a hot bath, shower or get in a hot tub after waxing.
6. Do not go out in the sun or sunbathe, swimming.
7. Do not apply deodorant, or make up for up to 24 hours after waxing.

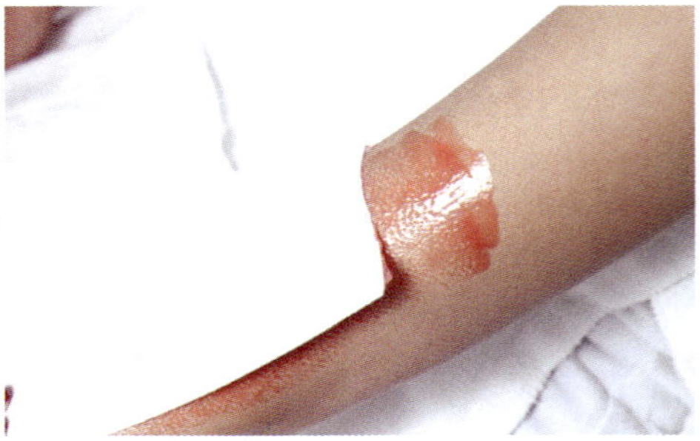

Be warned : The cotton strips used for waxing are a breeding ground for bacterial growth - no amount of washing is enough. Make sure the strips used are disposable ones.

Bikini Waxing

This is removing pubic hair with wax.

Do's & Dont's

1. Make sure you go to a licensed salon. The technician should be experienced. Do not hesitate to ask questions.
2. There should be at least ¼ inch of growth before your appointment.
3. Make sure the salon practices proper hygienic procedures. Waxing technicians always should wear gloves.
4. Demand that the wax used for you is fresh and the spatula is sterilized.
5. Be gentle to your skin for 24-48 hours after a bikini wax treatment.

Be warned : Please be aware that bikini waxing, if not done keeping in mind proper hygiene, can result in severe health complications.

Laser

This is removal of hair through laser technology.

Do's & Dont's

1. Remember to limit plucking, threading and waxing etc for six weeks before treatment.
2. You and the technician will need to wear appropriate eye protection.
3. Wear sunscreen for the following month to help prevent temporary changes in the color of the treated skin.
4. If blisters occur, please stop treatment and consult a dermatologist.

A Traditional Method for Stopping Hair Growth

Practiced by grannies! When a baby came into the house she was treated to a regular 'vatna!' Grandmama's swore by this method.

Vatna

½ cup gram flour (besan) or wheat flour

¼ tsp turmeric (haldi) powder, a pinch of salt,

enough milk to make a batter consistency

(i) Mix all the ingredients to get a batter consistency. Apply all over body and face. Leave for 10 minutes. Rub with upward strokes gently. Once done prepare for a cleansing bath.

EXFOLIATION

Including exfoliation as a part of your bathing routine, at least once a month, is a good idea. Worldwide, the popularity of loofahs, sponges and stones on your body can not be denied! Here is a traditional method to 'polish' and exfoliate your skin on the body and face to slough off dead skin and result in silky smooth velvet-ness...

Oat Meal Body Scrub

3 tbsp oat meal and milk to make a paste. Rub this paste all over your body for 2-3 minutes. Rinse off after a couple of minutes.

Olive Oil Polisher

Separately in two bowls, put ½ cup of warm olive oil and ½ cup of sea salt. Wet your skin. Dip a body sponge first into olive oil and then into sea salt and massage this mixture all over your body in circular movements. Rinse off after a thorough rub down.

Orange Peel Polisher

The orange peels are dried and powdered finely. The powder can be bottled. Mix 1 tbsp powder with enough unboiled milk to make a thick paste. Massage by rubbing it gently with an upward, circular motion for 1 minute. Rinse with cold water after 5-7 minutes.

Maize Polisher

Wash face. Do not wipe. Take 2 tsp Makki ka atta on your palm and rub it on your wet body and face for a few seconds. Wash off.

Husk Polisher

Sift ordinary quality chakki ka atta to get the husk. Mix 1 tbsp husk (bran) of atta (wheat flour) with a few drops of rose water. Apply on your body and face. Massage gently on your face with an upward, circular motion for 1 minute. Rinse with cold water.

PAMPERING YOURSELF SILLY IN THE TUB

If you are a bathtub person, then, you may just qualify it to be your stress buster gadget!

A hot soak, after a tiring day, is something almost magical. Be a grabber! Take some time off to fill the tub and relax. Now here we are not talking about just water and tub! Here it all about muted lights, fragrance, bubble baths and oils.

Start with

1. At least four towels at your side. An extra to rest your head.
2. A loofah, body sponge, pumice stone and any scrub to exfoliate & slough off dead skin.
3. Choose your favourite bath oils, bath salts, or bubble bath.
4. Indulge in skin vitalisers such as Papaya, turmeric, oats, orange peel etc. Rub-scrub away.

A leisurely bath relaxes tense muscles, irons out a creased brow, opens clogged pores, restores moisture to the tissues, and adds a healing dimension to your day.

In the Indus Valley Civilization in Mohenjo Daro, which existed over 5,000 years ago, archaeologists unearthed a large pool-like structure with steps leading down at both ends. This is believed to have been a public bath!

Make your own refreshing bath tub

Pour into bath water

1 tbsp coconut oil (can use almond oil too)

2 tsp any body wash or shampoo

1 tsp bits of orange peel, 1 tsp chopped fresh basil leaves

1 tsp table salt

2 tbsp flower petals (any of your favourite fragrant blooms)

(i) Soak and enjoy.

The queen's bath

In the olden times, legend says, queens were known to create special baths. The most famous of these queens were, Noorjahan and Cleopatra! Noorjahan loved to bathe in rose petals awash water. Cleopatra abundantly used goat's milk, honey, oats etc. to enjoy a good soak!

The Famous Cleopatra's Bath!

Run water at room temperature in your tub. Add a cup of full cream milk, 2 tbsp honey, handful of rose petals, a few drops of a fragrant essential oil, to the tub water. Dip your body into this and enjoy your bath!

Warm baths in a tub are known for some health benefits, like a release of muscle tension and also has a de-stressing effect. This bath is known to chase away worries and tensions replacing them with ease and relaxation

BENEFITS OF WATER

Dehydration

Leads to dry, wrinkled skin. Plenty of water keeps your moisture levels up.

Water is very good for your body because...

(i) Muscle consists of 75% water
(ii) Brain consists of 90% of water
(iii) Bone consists of 22% of water
(iv) Blood consists of 83% water

The functions of water in human body are vital. The water:

(i) Transports nutrients and oxygen into cells
(ii) Moisturizes the air in lungs
(iii) Helps with metabolism
(iv) Protects our vital organ
(v) Helps our organs to absorb nutrients better
(vi) Regulates body temperature
(vii) Detoxifies
(viii) Protects and moisturizes our joints

Drinking Water for Healthy Skin

Skin is intricately tied to the overall health of your body. When your body is properly hydrated, you'll look better and feel better.

Adequate water rewards you with...

(i) Enhanced health
(ii) Increased energy
(iii) Bright, clear eyes
(iv) A radiant complexion

In addition, bloating and puffiness often disappear.

Water...how much to drink?

Drinking 8 glasses of water per day is recommended.

Symptoms of Dehydration

Here are some of the symptoms that you need more water:

Dark Urine

Dark Yellow or Orange in Color: Urine is generally pale yellow to clear when you have sufficient water intake. Dark color or strong smell indicates that you need to drink more water.

Dry Skin

Skin is the largest body organ and requires its share of water.

Thirst

Thirst is the most obvious sign that you're already dehydrated. It is always a good practice to drink more water when your are not thirsty, don't wait until you're thirsty.

Hunger

Most people mistake hunger for the indication to eat more, whereas in actual fact, they may be dehydrated. So before you have your meal, grab a glass of water.

Fatigue

Water is a source of energy and gives you a boost in energy.

MAKEUPOLOGY

Did you know that Foundation can...

Slim Down a Broad Face

1. Put the matching shade of foundation all over the face.
2. A darker shade is applied on the broad jaw line and temples on a square face.
3. Blend the edges of the dark foundation with the fingers so that no patches, streaks or lines of demarcation show.

Slim Down a Broad Nose

1. Put the matching shade all over the face.
2. Put the darker shade on the places you want to camouflage, for example, the sides of a broad nose.
3. Blend the edges of the dark foundation with the fingers so that no patches, streaks or lines show.

Shorten a Long Nose

1. Put the matching shade of foundation all over the face.
2. Apply a darker shade of foundation just under the tip of the nose blending around half the nostril. Don't use it on the tip of the nose.
3. Blend the edges of the dark foundation with the fingers so that no patches, streaks or lines show.

Widen a Thin Nose

1. Put the matching shade of foundation all over the face.
2. Draw a straight line down the centre of the nose with a shade darker than yours and blend. Don't use it under the nose tip.
3. Blend the edges of the dark foundation with the fingers so that no patches, streaks or lines show.

Concealers

(i) Concealers come in shades to match every skin tone. These diminish the presence of pimples, marks and dark circles under the eyes. Concealers may be liquid, cream or solid (stick).

(ii) Moisturize your face first for easier application.

(iii) To prevent concealer from setting into fine lines, wipe away excess. Blot with a tissue for a matte finish.

(iv) Whether you're fair or dark, your concealer should also have yellow tones. It suits Indian skins better.

(v) Don't use a concealer that's white or more than half a shade lighter than your skin tone. Try for an exact match.

(vi) Apply before foundation. Set the concealer with powder.

(vii) Sometimes after the use of concealer, foundation may be avoided.

Shade of Foundation?

(i) A wrong choice of shade and incorrect application of foundation gives that unnatural or caked on look.

(ii) Select a shade matching your skin colour by applying a little on the jaw line (the side of your face).

(iii) Never test on your wrist. Your wrist is never the same colour tone as your face.

(iv) A light shade of foundation will give a chalky look, where as a dark shade will make you look darker. Choose a shade which blends well with your skin.

(v) Put a small dot on the jaw line and rub lightly to blend. A patch should not appear. This is the right shade for you.

Applying Blusher...

If You've Got a Wide Face...

Smile - see where your cheeks are rounded? Start at the centre and brush colour out towards eye and slightly up to the temple.

If You've Got a Narrow Face...

Smile - see where your cheeks are rounded? Start at outer half and brush out towards your ear on each cheek. With blush left on brush, apply a bit on the chin.

To Give a High Cheek Bone Effect

1. Apply the regular blusher in the hollow just under the cheek bone moving towards the upper portion of the ear which is near the temples.
2. Apply a lighter shade of blusher on the bone area to give a high cheek bone effect.
3. You may apply a little regular blusher to the nose, forehead and chin.

To Shorten a Long Face

1. Apply the blusher into the hollow of the cheek blending up to the sides.
2. Avoid the blusher on temples
3. Apply lightly on forehead to distract the length of the face and apply a hint on the chin to reduce length.

To Emphasize High Cheek Bones

1. Draw a line with a blusher two shades darker than your skin shade under the cheek bone in the hollow of the cheek starting in line with the corner of the iris of the eye and moving out towards the ear.
2. Blend the shade upwards, the darker remaining in the hollow.

All about Lipstick

Applying Lipstick

(i) First prime your lips with a good base of foundation and powder to remove all colour from your lips.

(ii) Outline your lips with a lip pencil - one or two shades darker than your lipstick. Define the centre curve on the upper lip with two precise strokes.

(iii) Continue the line of the upper lip, keeping your mouth closed and relaxed. Use short strokes, as they are easier than a continuous line.

(iv) On the lower lip, work from the centre to the corners.

(v) Work some lipstick into a brush and fill the outline of the lips. Work gradually towards the outline, don't cover it with a lipstick.

(vi) Open your mouth wide and brush the colour into the corners, so that there are no unfinished edges.

(vii) Blot with a tissue paper.

(viii) Touch up with some more colour. For a more natural look for the day time, blot again lightly with a tissue, but if you like the shimmer on your lips for the evening, do not blot after the final application.

TIP: You may also use the tip of your lipstick to outline your lips and then fill them.

Lip Colour

The lipstick must be applied twice. After the first application, blot with a tissue paper. Place the tissue on the mouth and press gently or press the tissue paper between the lips. After blotting the first application of lipstick, reapply. It stays longer by doing so. If you have dark lips, before applying lipstick, put some foundation and powder on your lips, so that you remove all colour from your lips. The actual shade of lipstick will now not change on your lips. A pink lipstick will now appear pink on dark lips too.

To Remove Lipstick

Always use cold cream to remove lipstick as this will help to soften and condition lips. After removing lipstick always dab on a bit of moisturizer.

LIP SHAPES

Want your lips to look bigger?

Try this subtle trick - Apply a Light shade of foundation followed by powder on your lips to remove the colour from your lips. Start with a lip liner pencil in a color that closely matches your colour of the lipstick. Make the out line just outside your natural lip line. Now fill with lipstick and then blend. How do you like your beautiful lips.

Want your lips to look smaller?

Apply a Light shade of foundation followed by powder on your lips to remove the colour from your lips. Start with a lip liner pencil in a colour that closely matches your colour of the lipstick. Make the outline just inside your natural lip line. Now fill with lipstick and then blend.

And more...

Using a matt lipstick will also help to make your lips appear smaller.

...Lip Tip

To get a good lip line, make an 'E' sound and keep mouth in this position while applying lip liner for outlining your lips.

Make-up : Colour Coordination

Matching and Contrasting

This is what colour coordination is all about. Make up should be worn keeping your dress colour and complexion in mind. The lip colour should not clash with your clothes and blush. A contrasting highlighter and shadow may be flattering.

With Pink Dresses

Shades of lipstick with a hint of pink and lavender look good. Cheeks should have a touch of lilac. The eye shadow may be in a shade of blue, contrasting with your dress.

Green Dresses

Take up browns well. Wear a deep brown lipstick or a brown with a hint of pink or orange, depending on what suits your complexion. A white or vanilla high lighter looks good, with a green eye shadow.

Yellow or Brown Dresses

Deep brown lipstick with a hint of orange normally looks good. Shades of pink lipstick are out! The blusher should have a peachish colour. Gold eye shadow is flattering.

Blue Dresses

Go well with pinkish lipsticks and blue shadow.

Important Cosmetic Tools

Some basic standbys will be invaluable for helping you achieve a professional, finished look to your make up.

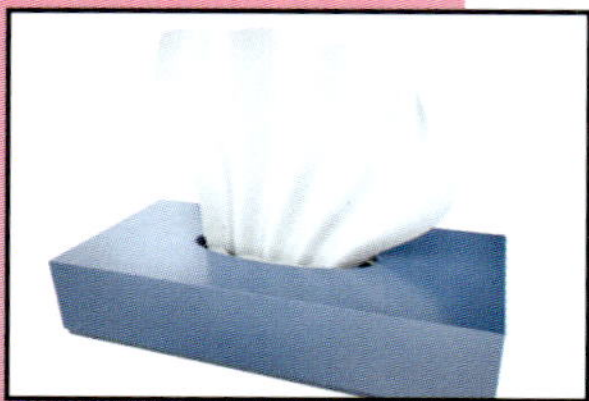

Tissues: Tissues will be needed for cleansing routines, for correcting mistakes, for blotting lipstick, and for keeping your hands and working surfaces clean.

Cotton Balls: Cotton balls is perfect for applying toner and for dusting off excess face powder or powder eye shadow. Cotton balls are convenient, but a roll will work out cheaper.

Cotton Buds: Cotton buds are handy for removing smudges, blending shadows, and softening pencil lines. They also make good applicators for powder eye shadow.

Powder Puffs: Powder puffs will be needed for compressed face powder.

Sponges: Sponges can be either natural or synthetic; it's good to have a stock of several for applying foundation. Clean and rinse them regularly.

Eyebrow Tweezers: Eyebrow tweezers, scissors, eyelash curlers, and a cosmetic pencil sharpener will all come in handy too.

Brushes: Brushes for make up come in all shapes and sizes. They are necessary for precision work around the lips and eyes, and also for applying light dustings of shader and powder eye shadows. Contour brushes are big, flat, soft brushes used for applying powder, powder blushers, shades, and highlighters.

Lip Brush: A lip brush is a chisel-ended brush, usually with a lid or a retractable head to stop it collecting dirt. Clean it by wiping off excess lipstick with a tissue and then rubbing in cleansing cream; wipe it clean with a tissue.

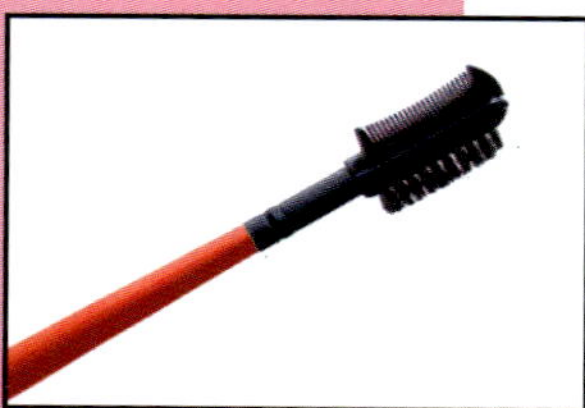

Sponge-tipped Applicators: Sponge-tipped applicators are useful for eye-shadow powders, or for applying colour beneath the eye.

Eyebrow Brush: An eyebrow brush is for training the brows into shape and for removing excess powder.

BEAUTIFULLY FRAGRANT MOUTH

Bad breath is a symptom of tooth decay! You need a dentist for that. However, we need our breath to smell good too! Indian meals are full of garlic, onions, sweet sticky mithai, that do not do well for your breath! Here is how you could keep bad breath at bay.

- Brush your teeth twice a day.
- In the Mughal times, the women would keep rinsing their mouth with rose water, diluted in 4 tbsp of water. A drop of clove oil, diluted with water, also was used to combat bad breath. Mint leaves, cardamom, basil leaves are all fragrant ingredients that help you to have fresh breath.
- A mouth freshener comes in the form of a paan. This is traditional way were a betal leaf is stuffed with cardamom, coconut, and betal nuts. However, too much of paan eating or even taking such aromatic masalas are harmful eventually. In Gujarat, mukhwas is served, which is a mixture of roasted fennel seeds, coconuts, melon seeds, poppy seeds, cardamom powder etc. Now this is a popular after meal mouth freshener everywhere!

- Mouth sprays or peppermint candy can stave off bad breath - but are not to be taken indiscriminately.
- Some believe that eating curd after a meal also diffuses bad breath.
- Chewing Gum is supposed to banish a foul breath as well as give your jaw an exercise! However be warned, the sugar in chewing gum could add kilos to the rest of your body, so chew in moderation!
- Fresh and good breath is also connected to a good digestion system. Make sure you are eating enough roughage, drinking enough water to keep your digestive system clear and healthy.

Sparkling Teeth

Rub teeth once a week

with lemon juice mixed with a little table salt

OR

table salt mixed with a few drops of mustard oil

OR

soda bicarb (baking soda)

Any of these will give a sparkle to your teeth.

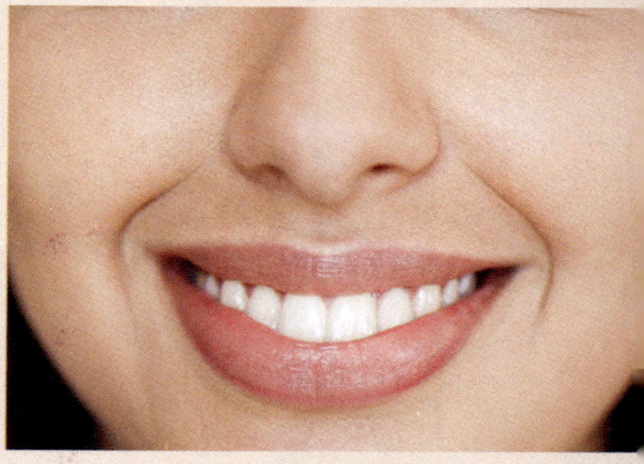

PRETTY HANDS & SOFT FEET

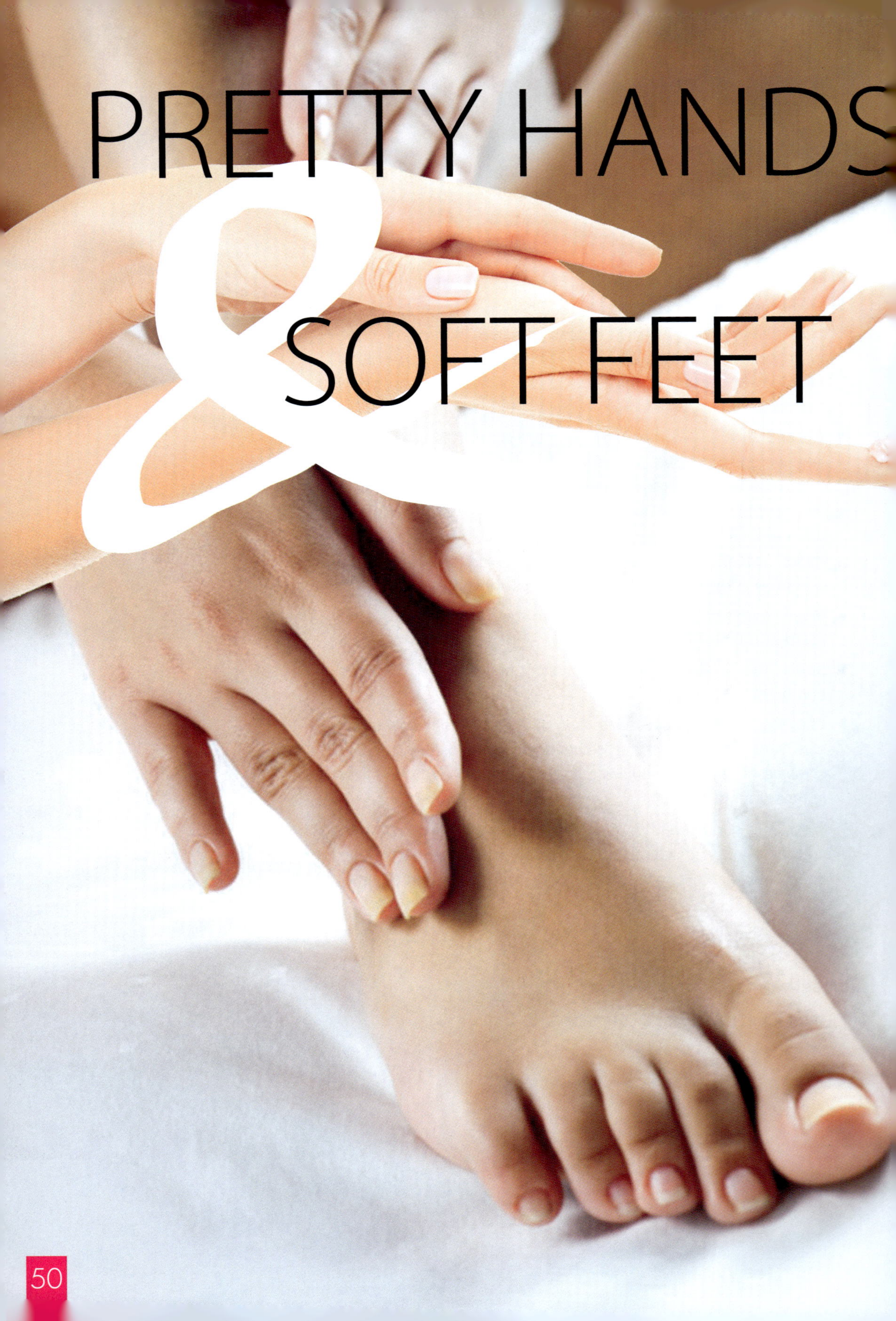

PRETTY HANDS

- The hand care extends to the elbows. Remember to scrub them while taking a bath. Apply a good herbal moisturizing hand cream morning and night.
- Keep a nail file in your hand bag. You could keep your nails in shape while commuting without wasting any time. File in one direction always. Push back your cuticles (the skin from where the nail starts) to give length to your nails. Before applying nail polish, push cotton wool pads between the toes to avoid smudging.

- Once a week dip your hands in warm water to which a little shampoo is added. Add 1 tsp of olive oil and ½ tsp haldi (turmeric) powder to the water. Scrub your fingers and nails with a nail brush. Clean the edges of the nails by rubbing with a piece of lemon. Lemon has a mild bleaching effect where as haldi softens the skin. Wash your hands after 10 minutes and massage the hands with the hand lotion.

- Smoothen your hands, by applying a little curd on them. Rub the hands for a minute together with curd on them, as if you are washing them. Wash off. When you apply your face mask, pamper your hands also with a bit of the same mask. Your hands get clean, soft and smooth.

Hand Lotion

A nongreasy lotion which repairs the damage done by house work.

MIX

3 tbsp rose water, 2 tbsp lemon juice, 1 tbsp glycerine

1. Mix all together and store in a refrigerator. Rub a little on your hands every night.

Moisturizing your hands

- Vitamin E is recommended to keep hands wrinkle free.

Hand Facial before bed time

Rub your hands with creamy facial mask.

Olive Oil & Malai Mask (suggested for hand care)

MIX

1 tsp olive oil or almond oil, 2 tsp fresh malai

1. Apply on hands with a brush. Massage for 2 minutes in the upward direction. Leave for 10 minutes.
2. Wash with warm water. Remove excess with cotton wool pads soaked in warm water. Pat dry.
3. Massage with petroleum jelly. Wear cotton or any soft cloth gloves for one hour. Remove and go to bed.

Winter care for hands

- Deficiency of moisture is the culprit that dries out your hands in the winter months also affects your nails and cuticles, which, though they've got absolutely nothing to do with wrinkles, can help with making hands look unattractive. Keep a cuticle cream beside your bed and rub in a small amount before going to bed.
- Milk. Just soak hands inside a bowl of warm milk for 10 minutes, rinse and moisturize.
- During the cold weather months make sure you wash your hands with just a mild soap. In fact, if the hands are very chapped and cracked, it's a wise decision to utilize the same cleanser (moisturizer, too) you utilize on the face.
- After washing your hands , don't dry them fully ... and apply a moisturizer (it'll lock in the water).

It is believed

(i) Deficiencies in Vitamin B can cause ridged nail beds. Lack of calcium can result in brittle and dry nails that chip off easily. For this purpose, be sure to eat foods high in these vitamins or take supplements to improve the look of your nails.

(ii) Use gloves while washing dishes and clothing and also heavy duty chores such as gardening.

(iii) One of the best ways to avoid fungal infections is to keep the hands warm and patting it dry after washing. Coldness of hands often affects the body's immune system by leading to illnesses such as influenza and sore throats.

(iv) Exposure to the sun leads to damage of skin. Thus it is recommended that you use a sunscreen lotion or sun-block cream before venturing out.

SOFT FEET

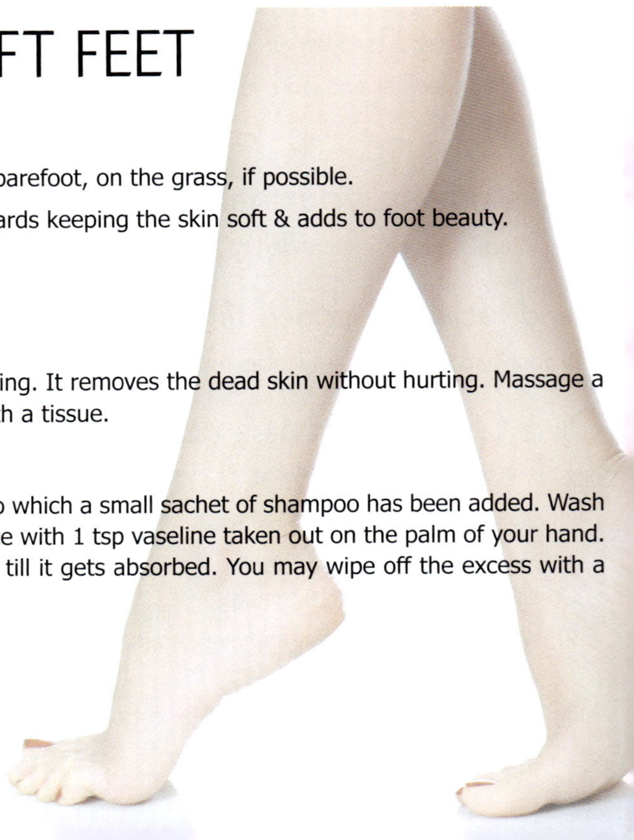

Feet Care...

- The best exercise for the feet is walking barefoot, on the grass, if possible.
- Creaming feet daily goes a long way towards keeping the skin soft & adds to foot beauty.

Cracked Feet turn Baby Soft

MORNING ROUTINE...

Rub heels with a pumice stone daily while bathing. It removes the dead skin without hurting. Massage a good hand and body lotion. Remove excess with a tissue.

BED TIME ROUTINE...

Before going to bed, soak feet in warm water to which a small sachet of shampoo has been added. Wash after 10 minutes. Mix a few drops of lemon juice with 1 tsp vaseline taken out on the palm of your hand. Rub this lemon-vaseline into the cracked heels till it gets absorbed. You may wipe off the excess with a tissue.

Must do

Moisturizing foot scrubs and exfoliators also help remove dead skin. After you scrub, apply a rich foot cream or balm containing shea butter or cocoa butter.

Apply balms or heel creams containing salicylic acid or urea to soften tough calluses.

If your heels are very dry and cracked, see a podiatrist or dermatologist for a prescription treatment. If they're not that bad, there are plenty of moisturizing products from which to choose.

Petroleum Jelly draws moisture into the skin. To moisturize your toenails, use a cuticle cream, petroleum jelly, or vitamin E oil. Put it over the entire nail, including the cuticle, and gently rub it in.

Tired Feet

(i) Bathe tired feet in a basin of hot water with 2 tablespoonful salt or 2 tablespoons of vinegar dissolved in it.

(ii) Rub glycerine on tired feet at bed time and by next morning you will find them fresh and supple.

Feet/Sole with Cracks

- Mix equal quantities of glycerin and lemon juice. Apply every night before going to bed. This mixture can be made and stored in a glass bottle.
- Massage your feet with castor oil every night (in winters) for 2-3 minutes & then wear socks at night.
- Grind equal amounts of neem leaves & turmeric (haldi). Apply on affected area.
- Finely grind a handful of henna leaves. Add 2 tablespoons lemon juice and apply on the feet.
- Mix the juice of bottle gourd (lauki) and sesame oil (til ka tel) in the ratio 4:1 and heat till all the moisture has evaporated. Bottle and use over cracked skin.

Be Warned

A simple trip to the parlour could land you in the hospital emergency room, read on to find out how...

Fish Pedicure

Garra Rufa! Very nice and pleasant if done in sterilized conditions. Any cut or sore on your foot can cause major infections if you go in for such a pedicure.

Safety Mantra : Reschedule appointment and go only when the cuts have been healed.

Manicure and Pedicure

Manicure and pedicure is so common! Very much needed too! But did you know that if the instruments are not sterilized you may be exposed to infections like warts, hepatitis C and staph infections.

Safety mantra : Make sure the instruments are properly sterilized. Ask manicurist/pedicurist to wash their own hands, as well as making sure that their area is clean! Everything that is used, not just the nail tools, have been properly cleaned, including the foot bath and the bowl for the soapy nail soak.

SHOES & YOU

Buying shoes is a serious business! Unfortunately many of us ignore the importance of fitting a shoe right...

Foot pain is very common. It is believed that the average person walks up to 115,000 miles in a lifetime, which is about four times around the world! Each foot hits the ground around 1,500 times every mile, so you do the math and figure out how many times your feet strike the ground in an average day.

Most people tend to buy shoes that are fashionable and don't really care about the torture they are giving their feet!

Keep in mind when buying shoes...

- There should be enough room for your heel to move but not slip
- The space between the end of your big toe and the tip of the shoe should be a thumb's width
- Your foot should never be wider than the shoe
- Try on shoes at the end of the day or after exercise because that is when your feet will be the largest
- Wear the same kind of socks that you will be wearing when you exercise when you try on your shoes
- Your foot should fit comfortably without stretching the upper part of the shoe over the middle of the shoe.

Foot Fuss...

Wearing heels feels great but reserve them for formal dos! Try and wear comfort shoes as much as you can.

Relax those feet

(i) Encourage professional foot massages for yourself – making sure you are getting hygienic service.

(ii) Move your ankles and wiggle your toes to relax them.

(iii) When at a sit down dinner, kick off your shoes and relax your feet.

(iv) Warm saline foot baths after a long tiring day does wonders for you and your feet.

Did You Know Wearing Badly fitting, Tight Shoes Cause...

(i) Corns

(ii) Callus

(iii) Blisters

(iv) Bunions

(v) Foot pain

(vi) Heel Pain

(vii) Knee joint pain

(viii) Back aches

'Dadi Maa Ke Nuskhes' for foot corns...

- Tie a fresh slice of lemon over the corn (painful area) and keep it all night.
- Massage castor oil on the corns every morning and night before sleeping. Massage for 2-3 minutes so that the oil gets absorbed. In 3-4 weeks the corns will disappear.
- Mash 1-2 cloves & garlic and tie over the corns. Keep overnight.

When Buying Heels...

(i) Stand up in the heels and see if there is a gap in the back of the heel between the shoe and your heel.

(ii) Wiggle your toes. If you have wide feet, avoid pointy-toed shoes to keep your feet from being scrunched.

(iii) Observe your toes, if you have open-toed heels on. Your toes should end a quarter inch away from the edge of the sole. More or less space means the shoes are too big or small.

(iv) Run your finger along the arch of your foot. If the shoe gaps unattractively, you need a narrower shoe; if it is tight and rubs your instep, you need a wider one.

Shoe Trivia

(i) In Biblical times a sandal was given as a sign of an oath.

(ii) In the Middle Ages, a father passed his authority over his daughter to her husband in a shoe ceremony. At the wedding, the groom handed the bride a shoe, which she put on to show she was then his subject.

(iii) Wooden shoes mounted on thin blocks 3 to 4 inches high were worn for centuries in Japan. Shoes were selected traditionally with an ear for the sound made by the wooden blocks when walking.

(iv) Six-inch-high heels were worn by the upper classes in seventeenth-century Europe. Two servants, one on either side, were needed to hold up the person wearing the high heels.

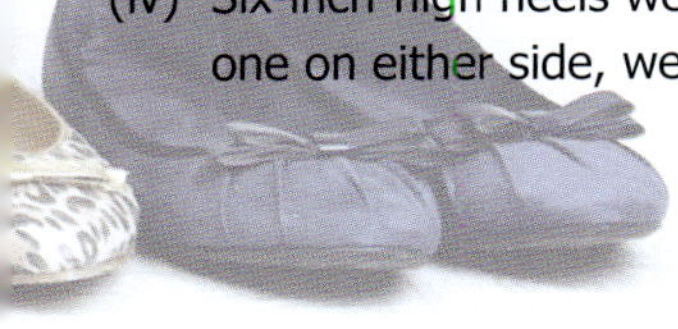

DRESS RIGHT

FEMALES IDENTIFY YOUR BODY SHAPE!

Identify your shape and have a counseling with your local boutique or designer and know what sort of outfits you should choose for yourself. This is half the battle won whilst dressing right!

Apple Shaped

This is when you are round in shape more graphically put: An ample bust, rounded stomach and slimmer hips.

Pear Shaped

Thin on top and bigger lower body! This means a small bust and narrow shoulders, and bigger hips, thighs or buttocks- you've got a pear body shape.

Strawberry Shape or inverted triangle

This is when you are top heavy and slimmer down below. If your shoulders are broader than your hips, you're the inverted triangle body or strawberry shape.

Hourglass Shape

This is when your body is marked by proportionate curves. Bust-hip same size more or less- with a slim waist.

Rectangle Shape

Or Athletic or slender body types. Rectangle body shapes are characterized by straight lines – that is waist, hip and shoulder widths in inches are all parallel to each other.

Suggestion on what clothes to choose...

Apple Shape

Safely wear fulsome floaty tops that skim down to the waist. Opt for an empire waist shirt that begins under the bust to draw attention away from the stomach. Never wear skinny trousers.

Pear Shape

You need to define your waist area so find clothes that do that. These are belted or cinched styles that compliment your midriff. Get skirts with a slight a-line cut. Nice slightly flared kurtis are good for you. Say a big No to tight skirts, trousers and salwar suits.

Strawberry Shape

You need to have a fitted bodice that flares at the ends. Fuller skirts and wide leg trousers will balance out your body shape beautifully. Don't be afraid of bright colour on your bottom half.

When making sari blouses or even salwar suits avoid puff sleeves, epaulettes and halter-necks.

Rectangular Shape

Here you need to fashion out curves! For you it is generally recommended to wear scoop-neck and sweetheart tops! Belt your waist to create more of an hourglass figure. Wear tops with collars, ruffles and details to give a top fuller look.

Hour Glass Shape

Wear Indo-western clothes that define your waistline too. Avoid stiff bulky clothes and baggy styles. Should choose figure hugging or semi figure hugging clothes that accentuate your curves.

Dressing for Work Fashionably

1) Please ask yourself these questions: Where is my work place located? How am I getting there? What is appropriate for me to wear?
2) If you are taking public transport then best would be to dress for comfort with style. Combine trendy kurtas with patialas, dhoti salwars or even readymade churidhars and manageable duppattas. If you prefer westerns then in summer you need to wear comfy cotton trousers with airy tops! Most women opt for full sleeve shirts even though it is warm-this works as an ideal sun protection scheme!

   In winters wear smart jackets over trousers. Combine your warm shirts etc to match. Jackets look miles better than sweaters and pullovers. Wear simple accessories. Most of all wear comfy foot wear.
3) If you are dressing for a corporate office a business suit does well. It can be a trouser suit or even a slim cut skirt. Merge a same colour suit with a feminine shirt. Wear little jewelry. Shoes mostly are closed ones. Choose your heels to how comfy you want to be!
4) Also in order to not bring attention to yourself please do not wear anything that is ill-fitting or too large. When choosing work outfits, stick to items with a contemporary cut! So avoid dowdy clothes. To allow long hair, to be manageable please put it up. A business suit and a chignon hair style compliment each other greatly.
5) Trendy does not mean something you would wear at a party or lounge! Choose confidence building clothes. Like a colour that suits you. A style that compliments you. This actually gives a boost to your confidence through the day.

How to Dress Right?

1) Buy what suits you and not what is in fashion
2) Be very careful in matching your jewelry. So go with one of these styles: Long earrings with small or no neck piece – or – big ring with small bracelets.
3) Do not over dress. A simple black number can be high-lighted with just a huge ring, and good shapely shoes! Carry a bright clutch purse! Do not forget the appropriate make up, well brushed hair and a confident attitude.
4) Subtle dressing gives off an elegant sophistication. If you are wearing say a pink chiffon sari, for a lunch date, wear pink pearls, light nude look make up and a big white bag with white heeled shoes. If you are wearing a high neck brocade salwar suit for an evening soiree, then try and match jewelry smartly to avoid looking stuffy and boxed in!

2 REASONS WHY IT IS IMPORTANT TO DRESS RIGHT...

1. If you are wearing an outfit that gets you many compliments your confidence soars!
2. Very often wrong dressing causes an eye sore vision for whoever has to see you!

A smart business suit looks good at work.

PERFUMED

Natural scents

Ancient India saw women using scents from natural resources. Chandan or Sandalwood from a tree or rose petals from blooms were used to apply fragrances. Sandalwood sticks would be burnt so the smoke coated the person with fragrance! These essences are still used even today! Many roll their hair with jasmine flower strands to smell fresh! Lavender, Marigold all have inspired great smells.

Perfume is a person's best friend! After a bath, a clean scrubbed skin, needs a good odour, so we all agree! A good perfume, gives you a great feeling! It is believed that the perfume you choose also divulges your personality traits! Perfume, however, should be chosen with care. Some times people need specified smells for their skin types. Using testers, with patience, works out which smell suits you the best!

Research says, 'In 2005, archaeologists uncovered what are believed to be the world's oldest perfumes in Pyrgos, Cyprus. The perfumes date back more than 4,000 years. The perfumes were discovered in an ancient perfumery. At least 60 stills, mixing bowls, funnels and perfume bottles were found in the 43,000-square-foot factory.

In ancient times, people used herbs and spices, like almond, coriander, myrtle, conifer resin, bergamot, as well as flowers.

The word perfume used today derives from the Latin word 'per fumum', meaning "through smoke." Perfumery, or the art of making perfumes, began in ancient Mesopotamia and Egypt and was further refined by the Romans and Persians.

The world's first recorded chemist is considered to be a woman named Tapputi, a perfume maker who was mentioned in a cuneiform tablet from the 2nd millennium BC in Mesopotamia. She distilled flowers, oil, and calamus with other aromatics, then filtered and put them back in the still several times...'

How to Apply Perfume

After a shower and a towel rub down, spray your favourite deodorant under your arms. Splash cologne behind your knees. Now wait a few minutes before you wear your clothes. Once you are dressed spray/dab your perfume on your pulse points.

Avoid rubbing the wrists together after application, to prevent 'crushing' the scent.
It is believed : always apply perfume before putting on your clothes and jewelry. Some scents tend to leave permanent stains on fabrics, metals, and pearls.

Give your fabric a patch test! In a hidden part of fabric, spray some of your perfume. If it stains, avoid spraying.

Smelling Fresh after using perfume is also a technique...

(i) It's awful when some people deodorize themselves to camouflage their 'not taken bath' status. "Sweat and heavy perfume can be so over powering!

(ii) Yes, perfume is considered the banisher of bad odour! Yet one should follow certain rules to emit fresh and appealing fragrance.

(iii) Apart from making sure you are bathed, the first step smelling fresh is to wear clothes that allow your skin to breathe.

(iv) Under-arm hair traps bacteria that act on perspiration and give rise to a typical, unpleasant smell. Use your deo on a de-fuzzed under-arms to carry the pleasant scents longer.

Why Pulse Points?

(i) The 'pulse points' are locations on the body where the blood vessels are closest to the skin.

(ii) These points gives off heat, which can help fragrance to float from your skin into the air.

(iii) Apply your perfume to the inner wrists, the base of the throat, behind ear lobes, in the cleavage, behind knees, and the inner elbows.

The cotton ball vapour!

If you are wary of using perfume on your clothes then try the cotton ball trick. Roll a small bit of cotton into a ball. Keep it on your palm and spray your perfume on it. Tuck the cotton into the side, (unseen), of your bra.

BEAUTIFULLY *Pregnant*

EATING FOR A HEALTHY BABY

During pregnancy, more than ever, it is essential that you have as varied and balanced a diet as possible. You do not need to plan this specially, nor do you have to eat for two. All you have to do is eat a variety of fresh, unprocessed foods, to ensure that you and your baby get all the nutrients you need.

IRON

Iron is absorbed more easily in presence of vitamin C. The tannin and caffeine present in tea and coffee lower iron absorption. Avoid drinking tea or coffee immediately after meals, especially if you are a vegetarian since you cannot eat the most easily absorbed sources of iron.

Foods high in iron: Red meats, oily fish such as sardines, poultry, eggs, spinach, cereals, pulses and legumes, dried fruits, olives, beans, whole meal bread.

PROTEIN

Protein helps to build, repair and replace the tissue, fights infection and helps in blood clotting. Animal sources are rich in protein, but are also high in fat, so limit your intake of these, and choose lean cuts of meat whenever possible. Avoid half/semi cooked or raw eggs and make sure all eggs you buy are fresh.

Foods high in protein: fish, meat, nuts, pulses and dairy foods.

FIBRE

Foods rich in fibre should form a large part of your daily diet since constipation is common in pregnancy and fibre will help prevent this.

Fruits and vegetables are important sources of fibre as you can eat a lot of them everyday.

VITAMIN C

It helps in building a strong placenta and fights infection, and also helps in the absorption of iron. It is found in fresh fruits and vegetables. Supplies of vitamin C are needed daily, as it cannot be stored in the body. A lot of vitamin C is lost by prolonged storage and cooking, so avoid prolonged storage & eat vegetables raw in the form of salads.

Foods high in vitamin C: broccoli, guava, green chillies, lemon & lime, orange, grapefruit, strawberries, capsicum, asparagus & tomato juice.

CALCIUM

This is important to ensure a healthy development of your baby's bones & teeth, which start forming around the eighth week. You will need about twice as much calcium as normal.

Foods high in calcium: cheese, skimmed milk, yogurt, leafy green vegetables, canned salmon, tofu, broccoli and legumes.

FOLIC ACID

Folic acid is a B vitamin that is needed for the development of the baby's central nervous system, especially in the first few weeks. Try to eat vegetables lightly steamed or raw.

Foods high in folic acid: Spinach, broccoli, brussels sprouts, green beans, cooked kidney beans, chick peas, black beans, split peas, whole meal bread, breakfast cereals, hazelnuts.

ESSENTIAL FATTY ACIDS

These are vital for the development of your baby's brain, nervous system and retina.

Food high in fatty acids: Oily fish such as salmon and mackerel are the richest source. Nuts, seeds, whole grain cereals, and dark green leafy vegetables are other sources. Oils such as olive oil are rich in omega 3 fatty acids.

AVOID

SUGAR

Sugary foods, such as cakes, biscuits, jam, and fizzy drinks, are low in essential nutrients, & can make you put on excess weight during pregnancy. Try to get your energy from starchy carbohydrates, such as whole meal bread and pasta, and cut down on sweet things.

ALCOHOL

Avoid alcohol as it slows the absorption of folic acid which is an essential nutrient for the baby. Alcohol has no nutrition and unnecessarily adds up empty calories.

Choosing the Right Pregnancy Exercise:

Walking – Just about everyone can do it. There is no easier exercise to fit into your schedule. Don't forget all the walking you do counts, even if its walking 2 blocks to the market or 10 minutes while the dog does its business. Weather's not cooperative – do the mall walk.

Jogging – Experienced runners can stay on track, but you may want to limit distances and stick to level terrain or use a treadmill. If you weren't a runner pre pregnancy, stick to walking.

Exercise machines – Treadmills, elliptical and stair climbers are all fine. Adjust speed, incline and tension to a comfortable level. During the last trimester, machine workouts are too strenuous. Also you have to be more conscious of avoiding stumbles when you are no longer able to see your feet.

Aerobics – Experienced athletes in good shape can continue dance and aerobic workouts. Tone down the intensity levels and never exert to the point of exhaustion. Beginner – low impact aerobics or the water version uniquely suited to the pregnant set.

Swimming and water workouts – In the water you weigh just a tenth of what you do on land, making water workouts the perfect choice. Boosts strength and flexibility, but is gentle on the joints. Many pregnant women report that it eases swelling in the legs and feet and relieves sciatic pain. Just be careful walking on slippery pool side and don't dive.

Yoga – Encourages relaxation, focus and attention to breathing – so its just about perfect. It also increases oxygenation (bringing more oxygen to the baby) and increases flexibility making pregnancy and delivery easier. Select a class specifically tailored to expectant moms or ask your instructor to modify poses so they are safe for you. Avoid Bikram yoga – its done in a hot room.

Pilates – Pilates is similar to yoga in that it's a low-to-no-impact discipline that improves your flexibility, strength and muscle tone. The focus is on strengthening your core, which will improve your posture and ease backaches. Look for a class specifically tailored to pregnant women or let your instructor know so you can avoid pregnancy inappropriate moves.

Breathing – Believe it or not, you also get exercise credit for breathing – at least, if you do it right. Here's how to do it: Sit up straight and place your hands on your belly. Feel it rise and fall as you inhale (through your nose, unless its stuffy) and exhale (out your mouth). Concentrate on your breathing by counting. As you inhale, count to 4; as you exhale, count to 6. Try taking a few minutes each day to focus on breathing deeply.

Abstaining:

If you are abstaining from exercise on your practitioner's orders, you are helping the baby and yourself. Your practitioner will almost certainly restrict exercise if you have a history of miscarriages or of premature labors, or if you have an incompetent cervix, bleeding or persistent spotting in the second and third trimester; heart disease or a diagnosis of placenta previa or preeclampsia. Your activity may also be limited if you are expecting multiples, have high blood pressure, thyroid disease, anemia or other blood disorders, or a fetus that isn't thriving; are seriously over or under weight; or have had an extremely sedentary lifestyle up until now. In some cases arm only exercises or water workouts designed for pregnancy may be okayed when other exercises are taboo. Check with your practitioner for your pregnancy exercise protocol.

THE KEGEL EXERCISE, (named after Dr. Arnold Kegel), is a pelvic floor exercise. The pelvic floor muscles support the rectum, vagina, and urethra in the pelvis. Strengthening these muscles by doing Kegel exercises is said to help having a simpler birth. What are pelvic muscles? Pelvic muscles are the same ones used to stop the flow of urine.

Beauty Care during Pregnancy

Stretch Marks: Somtimes an unavoidable affect of being pregnant. To help reduce stretch marks, drink a lot of water, make sure you take any vitamins and nutrients recommended by your Gynecologist, and eat a balanced and healthy diet. Some recommend that you use a gentle skin brush or washcloth to massage the skin and increase blood flow to the area, which might help. Keep the skin moisturized by applying a natural applications like cocoa butter, vitamin E cream to your stomach and breasts. A daily massage with almond oil from early pregnancy will help to arrest the onset of stretch marks.

Acne/Oily Skin: One good note, if you already have acne, sometimes pregnancy actually clears up the condition!

However acne breakouts are known to happen during the first trimester. Consult your Gynaecologist about how to safely treat acne. Prescription acne medications have been proven to be harmful to use during pregnancy.

Prevent Acne: When using makeup opt for products that are known not to clog pores and causing breakouts.

(i) Use mild cleansers daily to remove excess oil and prevent breakouts.

Dry Skin

(i) Keep skin moisturized. Avoid hot bathes and showers and use mild cleansers that will not further dry out skin.

(ii) You can also get dry, itchy bellies from the stretching of the skin. Massage the belly with cocoa butter.

(iii) For sore, cracked nipples, instead of regular lotions and moisturizers, use special nipple creams and ointments.

Tired, Swollen Feet

(i) Moisturize and massage feet with a refreshing foot gel or cream that contains cooling ingredients like menthol, eucalyptus or peppermint oil.

Varicose Veins

(i) Avoid prolonged standing and be sure to get enough vitamin C in your diet.

Makeup Tips

(i) If you experiencing dry skin, use hydrating foundations or tinted moisturizers.

(ii) Use blusher to perk up tired complexions.

(iii) Be sure to get enough rest. If getting your full eight hours isn't an option (especially after delivery), use concealer under the eyes for dark circles. Take five to ten minutes to cover puffy eyes with cool cucumber slices, moist tea bags or cool compresses.

(iv) When using concealers, use a shade lighter than your foundation. Then apply foundation only on areas where you have not applied concealer.

(v) Remember to finish off your look with lipstick or lip gloss in a shade that you love.

Take care of yourself

(i) Be sure to get enough sleep and try relaxation techniques like meditation or take pre-natal yoga classes. Stress is a big beauty buster.

(ii) Your make up routine should be something simple. Try to bring it down to basics. Consider doing simply your eyes, cheeks and lips quickly, leaving off the foundation. In the first trimester, you're likely to feel very tired and cranky. If you're used to wearing make up, going without is likely to also leave you looking as green as you're feeling in your co-worker's eyes.

(iii) If you find that the glow of pregnancy is only radiating blotchy skin, or chloasma (the mask of pregnancy), you can alter that with make up. A nice foundation or concealer can help to hide the uneven tones and blotchiness. Remember not to use foundation over concealer as they tend to cancel one another out.

(v) Maintain the right weight: Some of us might just take due advantage of binging on anything because we're pregnant. But that does not mean you accumulate pounds of fat. This pregnancy fat is anyway not helping your baby grow. So, it is best you avoid too much junk food and stress on nutritious diet.

(vi) Home remedies are the best: Apart from cosmetics, you can try out a lot of home remedies.

(iv) When selecting make up be avoid products with harsh chemicals. You should also watch out for certain chemicals in make up because your skin absorbs chemicals from everything. Including those with mercury and vitamin A and its derivatives as these can cause birth defects.

(v) Make sure that you pick products that your skin can tolerate. Your skin may be more sensitive during pregnancy.

Dressing during Pregnancy

You do not have to dress or feel clumsy and big! Wear clothes that are comfortable and that accentuate your curves. Take cue from many pictures flooded with pregnant celebrities. Opt for pregnancy fashion clothes!

First Trimester

Opt out for anything that is too tight or clingy. Pick outfits that are silhouettes that flow over belly, hips, and thighs that can camouflage the few pounds you may gain in the first months. Recommended dress styles:A-line skirts, Empire-waisted tops and frocks, wrap shirts and dresses.

2nd trimester

Buy in a few items that will grow with you. Look for pieces that have details like ruching, tie-backs, buttons or gathering at the sides, and wraps, which will all let you adjust your clothing as your body grows and changes. This will also give flattering lines to your bump.

3rd trimester

Pair a tunic in a comfy knit fabric over maternity leggings. You'll feel comfy and stylish.

Wear an Empire-waisted maxi dress – an ankle-length flowing knit dress that you can wear even after the baby has arrived. Added benefit: it's so easy – throw it on and you're good to go!

Fashionably Pregnant

ACCESSORIES : Chunky necklaces and bracelets or a big bag (that might double as a trendy diaper bag) can really make a fashion statement, and they are things you can continue to wear post-pregnancy.

SHOES : An open design will keep your feet cool in summer and allow for some normal pregnancy swelling.

Buy maternity jeans that have adjustable waistbands. Suggested are Jeans with a bootleg style.. For pregnancies in the summer, a pair of cargo pants is another option that may be more appropriate in some climates. You can also opt for maternity jump suits.

Opt for maternity basics that you can wear every day.

Wear skirts made of stretchy materials. This accentuates your curves in a nice way. Choose a basic color that you can mix and match with several tops or is professional enough to wear to work with a blazer.

TOWARDS A FITTER YOU

Fitness takes time and persistence. Regularity is of utmost importance.

To look your best you need to be physically fit also. Trimming those calories can only happen if you manage in an exercise routine every day.

Being fit is important because it helps increase long term health benefits that prevent all sorts of diseases, when you are growing old. It also keeps your muscles active. Your muscles need to communicate with your central nervous system so your muscles keep fit and do not deteriorate. Unfit bodies are susceptible to problems like difficulty in breathing, artery blockage, fatigue, obesity, and more. A healthy lifestyle is a must for a beautiful you!

"These legs are meant for walking"...

Walking 1 mile briskly in 15 minutes burns approximately 100 calories. You must warm up by walking at your normal pace for the first few minutes before you start walking briskly. Gradually increase the speed.

Whilst walking the best tummy exercise is to hold your stomach in for about 6 seconds, every time you remember to do it. By doing it several times, the muscles will become firm.

Constantly think of how you look, walk tall, sit tall, always attempting to maintain a good postural position.

At every opportunity walk rather than ride.

Try this to tone your tummy...

(i) Kneel on the floor.

(ii) Place your hands flat on the surface. Your weight should be resting on your hands and knees. Keep a distance between your knees and hands. Keep your back flat.

(iii) Breathe in-pull your belly in.

(iv) Breathe out-push your belly out. Hold this for a count of four. Repeat 8 times.

Plan your meals...

Choose brightly colored fruits and vegetables when you are shopping. Adopt a rainbow approach when eating and buying vegetables and fruits. Different colours mean different vitamins and minerals and hence you get a variety of nutrients that your body needs. When you eat fruits make sure this fruit medley is not over flowing, but a single serving. Even fruits have calories! Buy green, red, yellow, and different coloured vegetables. If you have a green vegetable like spinach/beans in the morning, have red carrots for dinner. Choose vegetables which have a high water content like cauliflower, mushrooms, bhindi, capsicums to denser vegetables like carrot, pumpkin etc.

Think, execute and keep...

The power of the mind is tremendous! Close your eyes and peep into the future. Imagine the benefits you shall have adopting a healthy life style, which will help you cut flab, not be called obese and help you move on.

Try and have partners to keep you company in a charter of action. "I have decided to cut the extra kilos, shape up and look at life with renewed energy. "LETS DO IT TOGETHER!" should be your invitation call. Could be your friend or spouse. This way one of you will make sure the decision is kept and so is a check on whether it is being followed correctly too!

Tips to Cope with Stress...

(i) Stress is the main culprit for most of the body ailments. One should know the causes and how to handle them to enjoy a stress free life.

(ii) Keep busy with the activities you enjoy e.g. reading a book, walking, doing crossword puzzles - these can reduce stress. Any fun activity can lower your blood pressure, and reduce your stress.

(iii) A good laugh can break the intensity of a situation and give you some much needed perspective. When you laugh your brain releases endorphins that create feelings of joy. A sense of humor is a key facet in creating greater balance in life.

(iv) A warm bath is relaxing on its own, but the effect is intensified when you add some herbs to the water. Fresh herbs or essential oils can be used.

Dancing to your tunes...

Yes dancing is one big contribution to weight loss and keeping fit because it:

1. Peps calorie burn
2. Peps your mood
3. Keeps mind off food!

Dancing does not mean you have to be trained. Works even if you groove in twists and bends -consciously moving each part or joint of your body to the music. So all you have to do is put on some foot tapping tunes and stomp away the calories. Remember not to do moves that can harm your muscles though!

Go Classical...

All of us have seen the basic hand, feet and neck movements of the Indian classical dances. Lets copy them. Move your wrists, your neck , hips and even your feet that way. It is a fabulous workout. Not only does it bring fluidity to your limbs, it is an exercise you won't mind doing! But your mantra for starting any physical activity should always be "go slow".

Why jogging helps...

Running is very good for your health. It provides a great cardiovascular workout, strengthens and tones your muscles. Jogging makes the heart stronger.

It increases the capacity of blood circulation and of the respiratory system. All you need is a good pair of shoes and well fitted clothes.

Quick Exercise Programme that Makes You Come Alive

Devote 11 minutes a day to these simple but balanced exercises. These exercises require no equipment and very little space. The stomach should be relatively empty, so do not do them immediately after food. Mornings are best, but if you cannot do them then, do them any time, when you can take out 11 minutes comfortably. See yourself losing inches!

Exercise 1 : Toe Touching : ½ Minute

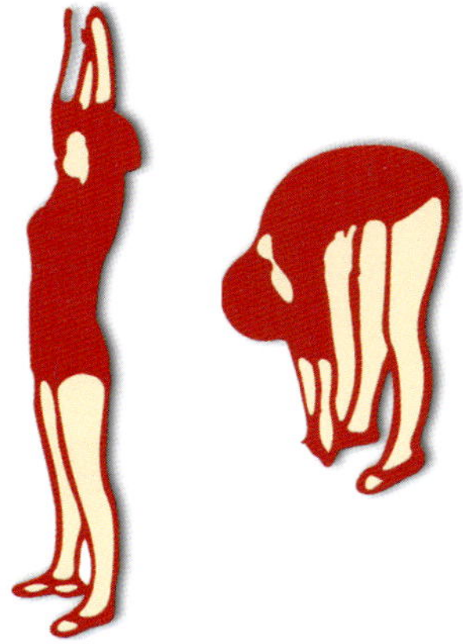

1. Stand straight, feet 12 inches apart. Keep arms straight over head.
2. Bend forward to touch floor between feet. Do not try to keep knees straight.
3. Return to starting position. Start by touching the floor 5 times and gradually increase to 10 times on the third or fourth day. This is a warm up exercise.

Exercise 2 : Knee Raising : ½ Minute

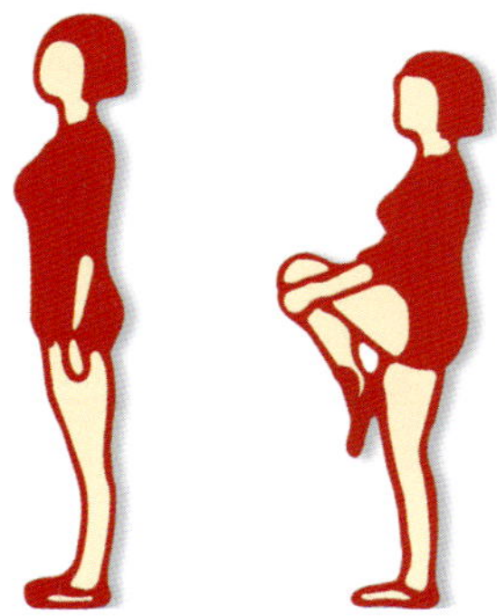

1. Stand straight, hands at sides, feet together.
2. Raise right knee as high as possible, grasping knee with both hands to balance.
3. Take the right hand to the bottom of the raised leg, just above the foot (shin). Hold tight.
4. Pull the raised leg towards your body, keeping the back straight throughout.
5. Lower foot to floor.
6. Repeat with right leg. Continue by alternating legs - left then right.

Note: Do it just 2-3 times in the beginning with each leg and then gradually increase the count to 10 with each leg. This exercise needs balancing so it looks tough in the beginning. Do it in front of your mirror.

Exercise 3 : Lateral Bending : ½ Minute

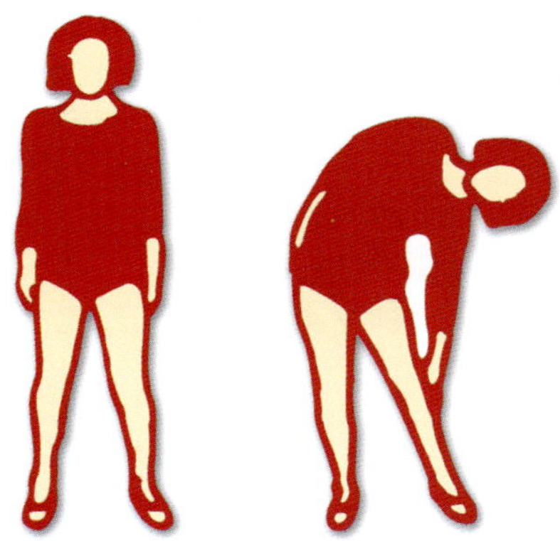

1. Stand straight, feet 12 inches apart, hands at sides.
2. Keeping back straight, bend sideways from waist to left.
3. Slide left hand down the leg as far as possible.
4. Return to starting position.
5. Bend to the right side.
6. Continue by alternating to left, then right.

Note: Start by bending 5 times to each side and gradually increase to 10 times on each side on the third or fourth day.

Exercise 4 : Arm Circling : ½ Minute

1. Stand straight, feet 12 inches apart, arms at sides.
2. Make large circles with left arm, making 5 forward circles and then 5 backward circles.
3. Repeat with right arm.

NOTE: This exercise is started with circling one arm at a time. When you get used to this exercise after 3-4 days, do more of this exercise. First make 10 forward and 10 backward circles with individual arms as explained above. Now make about 10 forward and 10 backward circles with both arms together at the same time.

Exercise 5 : Partial Sit-Ups : 1 Minute

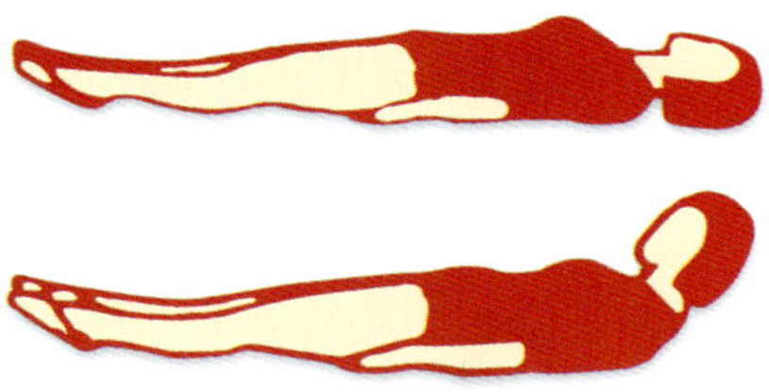

1. Lie on back, legs straight and together, arms at sides.
2. Stretch your feet, so that the toes are almost parallel to the floor.
3. Raise head and shoulders from floor until you can see your toes.
4. Lower head to floor.

NOTE: Initially do it only as many times which does not make you tired. Gradually increase, so that the head is raised 15 times.

Exercise 6: Chest & Leg Rasing : 2 Minutes

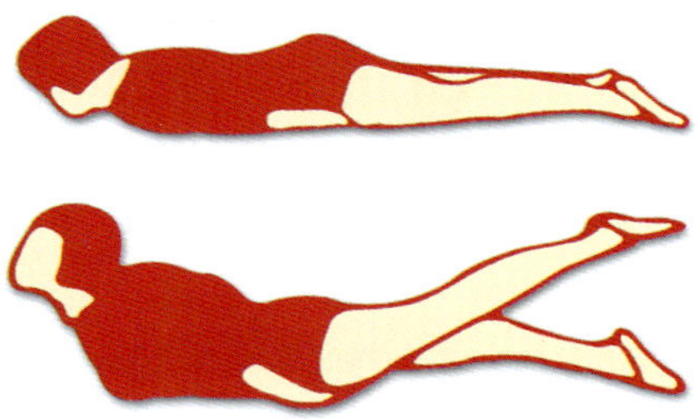

1. Lie face down, arms alongside, hands under thighs, palms pressing against thighs.
2. Raise head, shoulders, and lift left leg as high as possible from floor, keeping the other leg straight on the floor.
3. Lower the raised leg down to the floor.
4. Repeat raising right leg, head and shoulders.
5. Continue by alternating legs, left then right.

NOTE: Read the name of the exercise. It is the chest that has to be lifted from the floor and not the head. To lift the chest, the shoulders should be lifted properly. Gradually increase the count, so that after a few days, each leg is raised 10 times.

Exercise 7 : Side Leg Raising : 2 Minutes

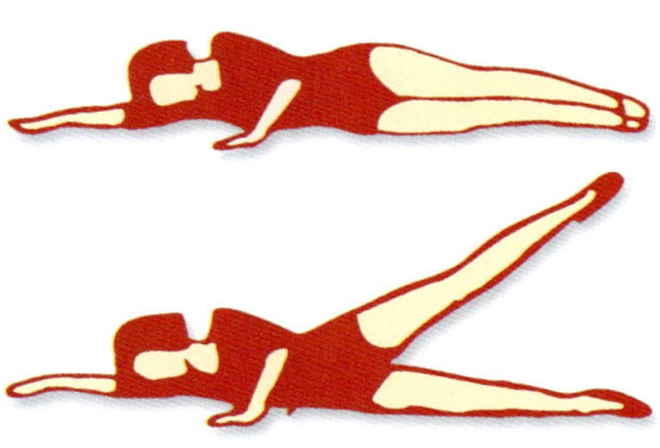

1. Lie on side, legs straight, lower arm stretched over head along floor, top arm on the side for balance.
2. Raise upper leg as high as possible.
3. Lower to starting position
4. Do this initially 5-6 times.
5. Roll to other side.
6. Repeat, raising the other leg.

NOTE: Gradually increase the number of times the legs are raised and also keep trying to take the leg higher as the days pass. If possible, each leg should be raised 15 times and till it is perpendicular to the floor.

Exercise 8 : Push-Ups : 2 Minutes

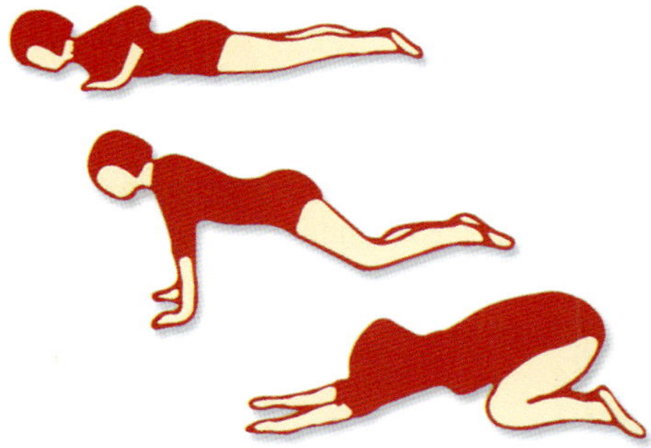

1. Lie face down, legs straight and together, hands placed directly under shoulders.
2. Push body off the floor in any way possible, keeping hands and knees in contact with floor.
3. Lower head to floor, stretching arms in front.
4. Return to starting position.

NOTE: Do the exercise very slowly, till you get the hang of it. Gradually increase the number of push-ups to 15. Place a small carpet under your knees, otherwise it hurts.

Exercise 9 : Leg Lifting : 1 Minute

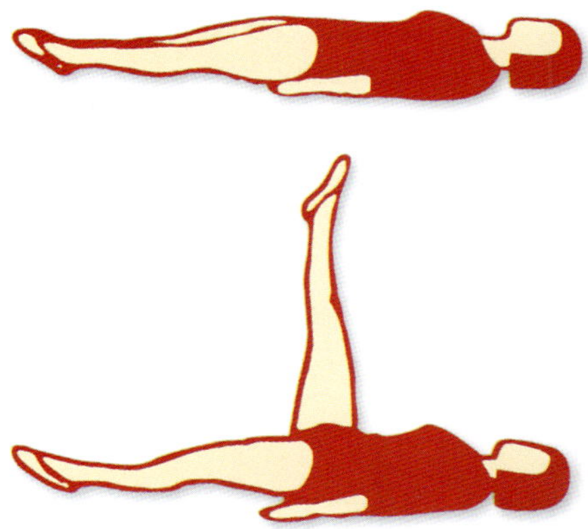

1. Lie on back, legs straight and together, arms at sides, palms down.
2. Raise left leg as high as possible.
3. Lower and repeat with right leg.
4. Continue by alternating legs, left then right.

NOTE: Do not strain yourself in carrying the leg very high initially. Do it slowly, trying to make the raised leg perpendicular to the floor as days pass by. Gradually, also increase the count to 10 times for each leg.

Exercise 10 : Run and Hop: 1 Minute

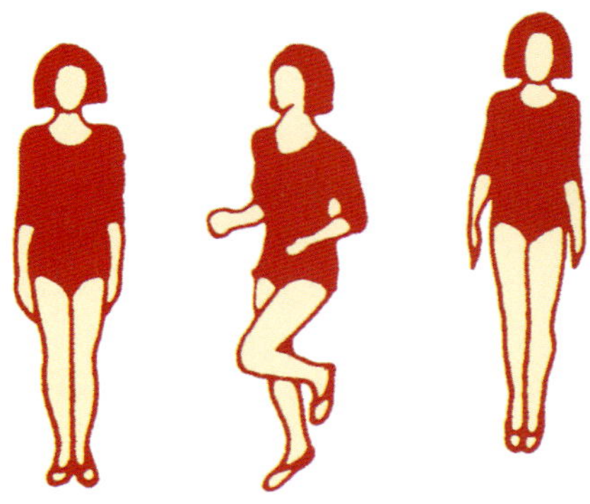

RUN

1. Stand straight, feet together, arms at sides.
2. Run in place raising feet as high as conveniently possible off the floor.

HOP

3. Raise both feet together off the floor. Jump about 4" off the floor, both feet leaving floor together. Jump continuously about 10 times for the first few days.

NOTE: Initially do this exercise till it does not fatigue you. Gradually increase the number of RUN to 100, counting each time any foot touches the floor. Try to Hop 30-40 times later on.

WARNING

Do not over exert yourself when starting to do these exercises. Remember to begin very slowly at first then gradually increase the pace. Think: NO STRAIN!

BAN STRESS...

Stress is the main culprit for most of the body ailments. One should know the causes and how to handle them to enjoy a stress free life. Stress could be due to conflicts in life, worries about problems or shortage of time. The body interprets these pressures as a threat to life. Too much stress can cause mental sluggishness and low energy.

These can be reduced by regular exercise and good social relationships. To forget and forgive is the key note to living a healthy and happy life.

Avoiding Stress

1. Take 10 deep breaths and concentrate on relaxing your whole body.
2. Yawning can help you relax by stretching the muscles, increasing the oxygen intake and releasing the tension. Yawn loudly and stretch your arms several times a day.
3. Nuts are a good source of vitamins and minerals that support the central nervous system and cardio-vascular system. These include magnesium and B vitamins. Eat nuts as a snack to combat stress and increase concentration.
4. Relaxation is a great remedy for stress. So people susceptible to stress should make time to doze every day. Lack of sleep leads to exhaustion and decreases your ability to manage stress. Take 6-8 hours complete sleep at night.
5. Massage induces relaxation and emotional well being, strengthening your resistance to disease.

Breathing Exercise for Anxiety

1. Sit on a chair without armrest, with your feet flat on the floor and thighs parallel to the floor.
2. Hold your back straight. Lay one hand over the other or place palms on your thighs comfortably.
3. Inhale through your nose and breathe deeply without forcing it.
4. Expand your chest fully and raise the shoulders slightly. Breathe in and imagine the air expanding your abdomen and chest in all directions.
5. Then slowly exhale through your nose and make sure that your exhalation took a longer time than your inhalation did. Repeat this for at least two minutes. Do it in a comfortable rhythm and do not strain yourself. Stay focused. Breathing deep and full can make the body completely relaxed.

Are You Eating Right?

Many health problems may just be due to your unhealthy menus!

Here is a look to check out the reasons...

Dry Skin

If you have an itchy, dry scaly skin not just in winters but also through out the year, it may signal a lack of significant amount of VITAMIN A.

Dietary Solution: Every time you go to the market, make sure your basket contains at least two orange or yellow and two dark green vegetables or fruits. Spinach, mustard greens, tomatoes, melons, mangoes, apricots, carrots and sweet potatoes all have plenty of beta carotene, which is converted to vitamin A in the body. You can also get this vitamin directly from whole milk, egg yolk, cheese and fish oils, but these sources have more fat and higher calories, so have less of these.

VITAMIN A will not only give you a glowing and sparkling clear skin but also, as a bonus, promote good vision. It may also inhibit the development of certain tumors and increase the resistance to infection in children.

Lifeless Hair

In extreme cases your hair can lose its luster due to lack of sufficient intake of PROTEINS & IRON in your diet especially if you are dieting.

Solution: First of all do not just blindly go on a diet. Eat a good mix of foods. Concentrate on eating more fiber and incorporate some exercise to lose weight wisely. If you are vegetarian, make sure you eat a mix of vegetables, grains and beans so you take in the balanced proteins you would normally get from meats. Iron is found in green leafy vegetables, peppers, cabbage, tomatoes, meats and eggs.

Fragile Bones

If you've broken more than a couple of bones during your adult life, it could be possible your bones are weak due to lack of body's chief bone builder that is VITAMIN D & CALCIUM. You are not alone if you go by the myth that only women need calcium as they age. In fact men also need it especially if they eat larger amounts of meat, which is high in phosphorus and increases the body's need for calcium.

Solution: At breakfast drink a tall glass of milk (skim or light milk can be a better choice), have a cup of low fat yogurt with lunch or dinner and sneak in green leafy veggies, beans and whole channa into your diet whenever possible.

A Racing Heart

If you feel your heart suddenly racing or fluttering for no good reason, its alarming. If it is accompanied by any pain or dizziness, consult your doctor, right now. But what if your doctor says that nothing is wrong and your heart still keeps racing or changing its pace at random, you may be suffering from deficiency of MAGNESIUM OR POTASSIUM in your diet.

Solution: Start your day with a glass of banana shake. A variety of leafy greens, pulses, beans and whole grains (wheat) during the rest of the day will ensure adequate intake of these trace minerals.

Eat for Beauty

Proteins

Proteins are needed for repair of body tissues. The skin and hair need enough protein and the deficiency causes dull and dry skin and scalp. Vegetarians specially need to plan their diets carefully to include protein rich foods such as soya beans, sprouts, cheese, paneer, milk, grains, peas & beans (rajmah).

Carbohydrates

Instead of sugar, add brown sugar or honey to your diet. Both help purify blood and cleanse the body of toxins. Say no to other refined carbohydrates like white flour (maida) and white bread etc., in which the nutrients such as vitamins and fibre get removed during refining.

Fat

You need very little fat, but a little fat is necessary for good circulation and supple & soft skin. So do not banish fat entirely from your diet. Choose sensible fat options in your meals

Vitamins

Fresh fruits & vegetables are rich in vitamins, the deficiency of which causes lusterless hair and a dull complexion.

Fibre

Fibre is very important. This indigestible carbohydrate is concentrated in the peels & rinds of fruits and vegetables and in the outer layers of grains and pulses. Fibre rich foods promote radiant glossy skin and clear eyes.

Beat High Sugar Levels in Your Blood by Including these in Your Menus

Beauty also entails keeping your insides in top condition. When following certain diet and health regimes, why not try and control sugar in your blood too. Instead of going on a completely sugar-free diet, now beat blood sugar by putting these on your plate...

Apple Peel: Apply peels have sugar reducing powers. They contain quercetin, a flavanoid that has anti-oxidant effects that helps in reducing diabetes. So when snacking on the fruit, remember to eat it whole. Apples come in many varieties. No matter which variety you choose, the benefits are equally high.

Asparagus: Asparagus is an excellent source of glutathione — an antioxidant compound that is known to keep blood sugar stable. The edible parts of the stalk are the shoots that appear underground, so choose those that are tender and green.

Beans: Most members of the legume family contain phytonutrients that are not only good for the heart but will also help you battle diabetes. The best way to take full advantage of these is by consuming dried beans that have been soaked in water for several hours before cooking. Think rajma, chole, etc.

Oranges: This perky fruit is not just another pretty looker about town. It's packed with phytonutrients that can help you fight diabetes including flavonoids, carotenoids, terpines, pectins and glutathione. It rates low on the Glycemic Index, which means it does not affect blood glucose levels highly, making the orange a good friend to have.

Broccoli: Broccoli is easily available at most speciality food stockists. It is an excellent source of quarcetin which will help you in your war against rising blood sugar. So blanch it for your salad or puree it for the soup.

Carrots: Have you heard of a rabbit with diabetes? It's probably because of all the carrots they munch. Jokes apart, these vegetables are not only good for your eyes, like your mother said, but also full of carotenoids that can help balance your insulin levels.

Nuts : Nuts are power-packed with minerals and healthy fats that protect your heart and balance your blood sugar. Go nuts!

Fish : Another great reason to dump red meat in favour of fish. Not only do the omega-3 fatty acids found in fish help fight depression, they balance your blood sugar levels and protect your heart.

Soyabeans : Also a member of the legume family, the soyabean is a complete source of potein, and also provides phytoestrogens, isoflavones and saponins that can help balance blood sugar.

Tea : Apart from being high on antioxidants that act as a cleanser for your system, here's one more reason not to miss out on your daily cup of chai. It has phytonutrients such as catechins and tannins that can help balance your blood sugar.

Let's go Nuts on Nuts!

Accused of being fattening, nuts are always eaten sparingly by some. However nuts are full of nutrients too! They should be included in our diet. Nuts are heart-healthy. Did you know studies show that eating nuts five times a week can cut the risk of a heart attack in half! With the onset of winters include a handful of nuts in your diet for a healthy you...

Buy raw nuts and toast them at home in you kitchen over a skillet. Roasting nuts in oil increases its calorie content. Packaged and processed nuts have unhealthy seasonings, sweetness and preservatives mostly. Try eating home toasted raw nuts if possible. A handful of nuts assures you of an intake of different vitamins and minerals.

Nuts can go rancid quickly. Unless you know you'll use up the family-size jar within a few months, buy a smaller container. Keep nuts in the freezer for up to six months; bring them to room temperature before using.

BEAUTY BULLETIN

Even if you want a non-made up look, mascara is a must because it defines your face and makes your eyes look brighter with just a single coat.

For removing dark circles : Take 1 tsp tomato juice, ½ tsp lemon juice, a pinch of haldi (turmeric powder) and ½ tsp besan (gram flour). Make a paste and apply. Leave for 10 minutes and wash off.

Rubbing ice over face before applying foundation makes makeup stay for long.

Make it a habit to use deodorant after a bath. It is a product meant for personal hygiene. Never share personal toiletries or products like deo roll-on or stick.

The right time to tweeze eye brows is immediately after a bath when hair follicles are open. This makes plucking less painful and easy.

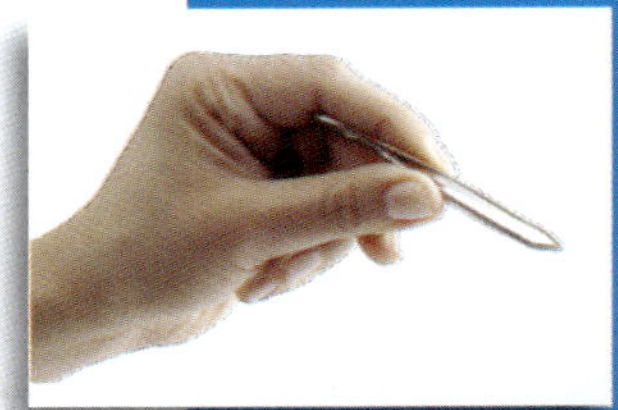

Pay for your manicure before you have it. That way, you won't smudge the nail polish while taking out the money from your wallet.

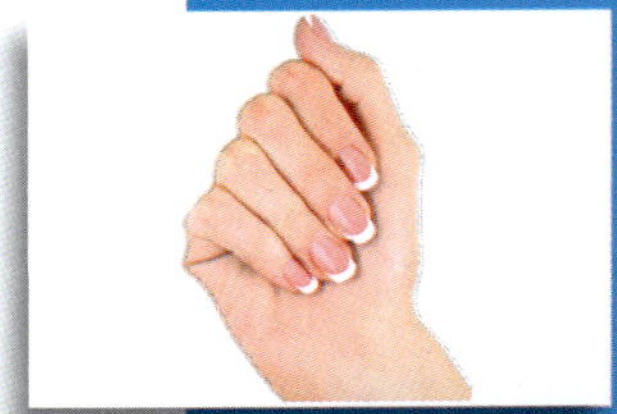

Know Your Body Type

Looking slim and trim is something we all aspire to be. But most times we have to identify our body type before we venture into any 'get slim' program. Most people even when dressing tend to follow trends, whether it is suiting them or not. Diet plans are thoughtlessly followed just to get to an image of oneself which may be far from reality. The point here is to follow any diet plan with the full idea of your own body shape. If you are on the plumper side, do not try and become drastically thin. Help your body lose inches so it is drawn away from obesity and jiggly stomach, towards being more toned and curvaceous!

Body types range from muscular, slim and curvy. Some women just need to trim on spot and really do not need to go for heavy dieting routines. Some women who are naturally slim need to eat right to be healthy. The diet plan given here is actually going to help you lose inches and not spiral your weight down dramatically. Why are we writing about a diet plan at all? Watching what you eat and keeping cravings for the unhealthy forbidden foods at bay is one of the major reasons for a fitter and a more beautiful you inside out! It is sometimes recommended to get a body analysis (BA) done to a certain what type of food have a sliming or fattening effect on your body type. Consult your trainer/nutritionist to explain how to get a body analysis done in reference to wanting to lose weight.

7 Days Menu Plan to Lose those Inches!

DAY 1

Warm a glass of water. Add ½ tsp honey and 1 tsp lemon juice. Mix and have first thing in the morning. 8 Calories

Bed Tea 40 Calories

1 cup tea with sugar free powder & less milk. 1 marie/monacco biscuit. No rusk.

Breakfast 215 Calories

3 tbsp (30 gm) wheat flakes or musseli. Add ¼ of a banana and ½ apple to ¾ cup milk and leave in the fridge for 5 minutes for the milk to become sweet. Add cereal and eat immediately. OR 2 toasted slices with cold coffee or a fruity shake made with a cup of toned milk and sugar free powder and lots of ice to make it upto a tall glass.

Mid Morning Snack 60 Calories

A fruit.

Lunch 295 Calories

Mixed vegetable curry made from boiled onion paste with 1 small katori of dahi/raita and one soya roti made with 1 part soya flour to 4 parts of wheat flour.

Tea time 100 Calories

1 cup tea with 2 fiber biscuits or some mixed nuts (3 almonds, a walnut, 4-5 raisins) or 1 toast.

Dinner 175 Calories

Celery and Tomato Soup

Spinach soya keema - recipe on page 95

Total Calories in a day = 893 Calories

DAY 2

Warm a glass of water. Add ½ tsp honey and 1 tsp lemon juice. Mix and have first thing in the morning. 8 Calories

Bed Tea — 40 Calories

1 cup tea with sugar free powder and less milk. 1 marie/monacco biscuit. No rusk.

Breakfast — 230 Calories

2 whole wheat bread slices stuffed with 2-3 tbsp home made paneer, made from 1 cup toned milk, ¼ small onion, ½ tomato and ½ green capsicum with green chillies. 1 glass of plain coriander lassi (3 tbsp dahi)/or a cup of milk/or a glass of cold coffee which has ¾ cup milk mixed with lots of ice to thin it down or a smoothie of less milk/yogurt and lots of ice and fruit.

Mid Morning Snack — 60 Calories

Papaya or an apple or orange or a guava - any seasonal fruit.

Lunch — 150 Calories

Mixed vegetables, 1-2 oat bran roti medium size

Tea Time — 80 Calories

One cup tea without sugar-2 monacco/marie biscuit or 2 tbsp bhuna channas or 2-3 almonds or a slice of brown bread with hari chutney

Dinner — 370 Calories

100 gms ready made tofu/paneer pan grilled in 2 tsp oil with lots of steamed or microwaved vegetables (include coloured veggies - green, red and white) hari chutney, no roti or rice.

Total Calories in a day = 938 Calories

DAY 3

Warm a glass of water. Add ½ tsp honey and 1 tsp lemon juice. Mix and have first thing in the morning. 8 Calories

Bed Tea 40 Calories

1 cup tea with sugar free powder and less milk. 1 marie biscuit.

Breakfast 200 Calories

Flaked Rice (poha) made with ½ cup poha, 1 tsp oil and lots of chopped coriander, french beans, cauliflower to make up to a bowl or 2 idlis with ½ katori of thin sambar.

A glass of plain nimboo pani.

Mid Morning Snack 60 Calories

A small plate of mixed fruits or water melon

Lunch 340 Calories

A katori of saboot moong daal or a zero oil curry/vegetable.

½ cup boiled brown rice with lots of vegetables- coriander, beans, capsicum, spinach, carrot, cabbage.

Tea time 6-7 pm 152 Calories

2 suji idlis with hari chutney OR murmure OR oil free namkeen (a small katori)

Dinner: SALT FREE 125 Calories

a big slice of papaya. Strawberry shake or cold coffee of ½ glass milk and ½ cup cold water. Sweeten with sugar free.

Total Calories in a day = 925 Calories

DAY 4

Warm a glass of water. Add ½ tsp honey and 1 tsp lemon juice. Mix and have first thing in the morning. 8 Calories

Bed Tea 40 Calories

1 cup tea with sugar free powder and less milk. 1 marie/monacco biscuit. No rusk.

Breakfast 176 Calories

a plate of papaya.

After 30 minutes of eating papaya -oat upma/oat pancake with hari chutney, avoid coconut chutney completely.

A glass of coconut water, ready made also will do or nimboo pani.

Mid Morning Snack 60 Calories

A kheera cut into sticks and sprinkled with some chaat masala.

You can have a whipped yogurt dip with it.

Lunch 275 Calories

Crispy quesidillas, recipe on page 98

Tea time 100 Calories

1 cup sugar less tea with some nuts or a piece of khandavi or dhokla.

Dinner 250 Calories

Nutri tomato platter (men can have a toast too with it).

Stuff tomatoes with cooked soya granules and bake.

After Dinner: optional 50 Calories

A glass of thin cold coffee/thin strawberry shake.

Total Calories in a day = 960 Calories

DAY 5

Warm a glass of water. Add ½ tsp honey and 1 tsp lemon juice. Mix and have first thing in the morning. — 8 Calories

Bed Tea — 40 Calories

1 cup tea with sugar free powder and less milk. 1 marie/monacco biscuit. No rusk.

Breakfast — 220 Calories

1 small glass of fresh tomato and celery juice (2 tomatoes, 1″ piece ginger and 1 stick celery) mix with ½ cup cold water, add 1 tsp lemon juice. Add kala namak or regular salt to taste.

Yogurt sandwich OR onion chutney and cucumber sandwiches made with 2 slices of whole wheat bread.

Mid Morning Snack — 60 Calories

1 plateful of mixed fruit chaat, include cucumber also in chaat.

Lunch — 285 Calories

2 grilled mushroom olive rolls, recipe on page 96

Tea Time — 100 Calories

1 cup sugarless tea with 1 fiber biscuit or nuts or 2 wheat momos or a piece of dhokla.

Dinner — 215 Calories

Broccoli and walnut soup, recipe on page 90

Veggie tikka (mushroom, broccoli, cauliflower)

Total Calories in a day = 928 Calories

DAY 6

Warm a glass of water. Add ½ tsp honey and 1 tsp lemon juice. Mix and have first thing in the morning. 8 Calories

Bed Tea 40 Calories

1 cup tea with sugar free powder and less milk. 1 marie/monacco biscuit. No rusk.

Breakfast 150 Calories

½ glass fresh lauki juice (from 400 gm of lauki) or nimboo paani.

Vegetable dalia or 2 toasted sandwiches of 2 tbsp home made paneer mixed with 2 tbsp each of chopped onion, tomato and coriander.

Mid Morning Snack 60 Calories

Fruit of your choice.

Lunch 300 Calories

Grilled burgers with coriander mint chutney OR a SUBWAY SANDWICH with no mayonnaise or cheese, ask for light mint dressing.

Tea Time 200 Calories

Fruit chaat mixed with some cornflakes.

Dinner 120 Calories

A light fruit + veggie salad.

½ of a ghiya ki subzi without oil. Make subzi with ½ tsp jeera, ½ onion, 1 tsp ginger- garlic chopped, 1-2 tomatoes and any masala (subzi masala, chana masala instead of garam masala to make it tasty).

Total Calories in a day = 878 Calories

DAY 7

Warm a glass of water. Add ½ tsp honey and 1 tsp lemon juice. Mix and have first thing in the morning. 8 Calories

Bed Tea 40 Calories

1 cup tea with sugar free powder and less milk. 1 marie/monacco biscuit. No rusk.

Breakfast 210 Calories

a glass of tomato and carrot juice (grind 2 tomatoes, ½ chopped carrot, 3-4 mint leaves and ½ cup cold water. Strain and add little kala namak).

2 Hari Moong Chillahs with a very thin lassi made with 2 tbsp yogurt, 1 cup chilled water, roasted cumin and salt.

Lunch 250 Calories

½ whole wheat maggie with lots of vegetables (1 cup chopped mixed vegetables - beans, carrot, capsicum, cauliflower).

Pre Dinner at 7 p.m. 200 Calories

Sprout Chaat with just 50 gm (1/3 of a packet) of sprouts steamed and mixed with ½ cucumber,

½ boiled potato, 2 tbsp anaar ke daane or ½ onion, coriander and chaat masala.

Dinner : salt free dinner 100 Calories

Parfait as on page 96

OR a tall glass of thin shake or a thin smoothie.

Total Calories in a day = 808 Calories

PS:

Don't forget to accompany this 7 day diet plan with regular, keeping you fit, exercises. Even after you have chucked the diet chart try and continue to eat healthy as much as you can and also plan your life style that includes regular fitness routines!

Walnut & Broccoli Soup

Serves 4

2 tbsp walnuts - chopped

1½ cups (½ small) broccoli - break into tiny florets, ½ cup chopped spinach

1 tsp oil, 1" stick cinnamon, 1 cup milk

1 tsp salt and ½ tsp pepper, or to taste

1. In a pressure cooker heat 1 tbsp oil and saute the tiny florets of broccoli, spinach and cinnamon for 3-4 minutes on low flame.
2. Add 3 cups water and give 3-4 whistles. Remove from fire.
3. In a liquidizer or a small grinder, put chopped walnuts with ½ cup milk and blend them well to a smooth thin paste. Remove the walnut milk from the grinder and add ½ more cup of milk. Keep aside.
4. When the cooker cools down, put the vegetables along with all the water in the mixer and churn till it turns into a smooth puree. Strain the puree.
5. Mix broccoli puree and walnut milk together. Boil. Simmer for 2 minutes.
6. Add salt and pepper to taste. Serve hot.

Fruity Salad in Orange Dressing

Serves 3-4

½ cup cubed cabbage, 1 carrot - cubed (½ cup), ½ onion - cubed (¼ cup chopped)

1 tomato - cubed, ½ cup halved or chopped grapes or strawberries, ½ cup orange segments (pieces)

ORANGE DRESSING

¼ cup orange juice (fresh or ready made), 1 tsp lemon juice

1 tbsp olive oil, 1 tbsp mustard

2-3 flakes garlic - crushed, ½ tsp oregano, ½ tsp salt and pepper, or to taste

1. Mix all fruits and vegetables in a large bowl. Chill in the fridge till serving time.
2. Mix all ingredients of the orange dressing in a bottle. Close cap and shake well to mix. Keep aside.
3. An hour before serving, pour the dressing over the fruit and vegetable mixture in the bowl.
4. Toss lightly with two forks. Add more salt and pepper if desired.
5. Refrigerate till serving time.

Crispy Quesadillas

Makes 16 pieces

4 tortillas or very thin chappatis

FILLING

½ cup yogurt - hang for 30 minutes (4 tbsp)

½ cup grated paneer, ¼ tsp salt and ½ tsp paprika, or to taste

10 slices of jalapenos - chopped finely

1 green chilli - deseeded and very finely chopped

¼ cup cheddar cheese grated and ¼ cup grated mozarella cheese (mix)

1 cup finely chopped green capsicum or zucchini

6-8 mushrooms - wash, slice thinly and microwave for 1 minute

½ small onion - cut into rings, 6 tbsp ready made salsa, ¼ tsp salt, ¼ tsp pepper

1. For the filling, mix paneer and 4 tbsp hung yogurt. Add salt and paprika to taste. Add very finely chopped jalapenos and deseeded green chilli. Keep aside.
2. Mix raw zucchini/capsicum, onions and blanched mushrooms with salsa, salt and pepper. Check taste.
3. To assemble the quesadillas, place one tortillas on a clean plate. Spread with half of paneer-yogurt spread. Place half of zucchini and mushroom mixed with salsa. Sprinkle half of the grated cheese on it, especially at the edges. Cover with the second tortilla and press well to close the edges. Brush with olive oil.
4. To serve, put on a greased non stick baking tray with oil side down. Brush with oil on the top. Place in the oven at 240°C for about 10-12 minutes till crisp and brown patches appear. Cut into 8 wedges with a pizza cutter and serve.

Grilled Mushroom Olive Rolls

Serves 3-4

6 slices of white bread

mayonnaise - enough to spread

maida paste (1 tbsp maida mixed with 2 tbsp water) - to seal

1 tsp onion seeds (kalaunji) mixed with 3 tsp white sesame seeds

FILLING

1 tbsp oil

1 cup roughly chopped mushrooms, ½ red bell pepper - chopped

1 tbsp chopped olives

½ onion - finely chopped, 1 tsp finely chopped garlic

1 tsp deseeded and chopped green chillies

2 tbsp chopped fresh coriander

1 tbsp grated cheddar cheese, 1 tbsp grated mozarella cheese

½ tsp salt, pepper to taste

1. To prepare the filling, heat oil. Add garlic, green chillies and onion cook for a few minutes till soft. Add mushrooms and stir for 3 minutes, add red bell pepper and olives. Remove from fire. Add all the remaining ingredients of the filling and mix well.
2. Cut sides of bread. Warm each slice in the microwave for 10 seconds. Immediately with a rolling pin, roll out a slice with pressure to make it thin. Roll out the second slice also quickly. Now place one slice on the kitchen platform and place the second one slightly overlapping the first one. With a rolling pin, press on the joint to seal.
3. Join 2 rolled out slices using flour paste to get a long piece of bread. Roll out the whole bread again. Spread mayonnaise on the slices.
4. Put 1/3 of the filling at one end and roll up. Seal the end with flour paste.
5. With a butter knife, spread mayonnaise on the roll on all sides. Roll over sesame seeds mixed with onion seeds.
6. Preheat grill for 5-10 minutes. Cover rack with foil. Place rolls on it and put under the grill for 7 minutes, turn and grill for 2-3 minutes till golden and crisp. Cut each into 3 pieces with a sharp bread knife.

Spinach Soya Keema

Serves 4

¾ cup soya granules - soak together for 15 minutes

1 cup milk, 2 cups spinach (paalak) - shredded

4 mushrooms - grated, 3-4 flakes garlic, 2-3 sookhi lal mirch (dry red chillies)

1 tsp jeera (cumin seeds), 1 onion - grated, 1 tsp ginger - chopped

¼ tsp haldi, 1 tsp dhania powder, 1 tsp salt or to taste, ¼ tsp garam masala

2 tsp lemon juice, seeds of 1 choti illaichi (green cardamom) - powdered

1. Shred spinach into thin long pieces. Measure 2 cups of shredded spinach. Wash in several changes of water. Keep aside.
2. Soak soya granules in milk. Keep aside for 15-20 minutes.
3. Crush garlic and dry red chillies together in a small spice grinder.
4. Heat a pan. Add 1 tsp jeera to the pan. Stir for a few seconds till fragrant.
5. Add crushed garlic and red chilli paste. Mix and cook on low heat till garlic turns golden.
6. Add onion, cook till golden brown. Add ginger. Stir.
7. Add grated mushrooms & cook for 2-3 minutes, stirring continuously.
8. Add paalak, haldi, dhania powder, salt and garam masala. Mix well for 2 minutes.
9. Add soaked granules along with the milk. Bhuno for 7-8 minutes till dry.
10. Add lemon juice and powdered chhoti illaichi. Mix well and serve hot.

Fruit Parfait

Serves 6

1 cup yogurt - hang for 30 minutes in a muslin cloth

2 cups chopped papaya, ¼ cup milk

¼ tsp vanilla essence

¼ cup anar ke dane, 1-2 slices of fresh ripe pineapple

2 kiwi fruit - peeled and chopped, ½ cup sliced strawberries

2 tbsp strawberry crush or syrup - to coat the glasses

a big apple - for decoration

1. Put papaya in a mixer. Blend till smooth. Cook this papaya puree for 3-4 minutes on medium flame. Keep aside to cool.
2. Put hung yogurt, cooked papaya puree, milk and vanilla essence in the blender and blend again. Keep papaya whip aside.
3. Coat a narrow glass with ½ tsp of strawberry syrup or crush. Put 1 tbsp anar ke dane.
4. Arrange a layer of chopped pineapple pieces.
5. Put 1" layer of papaya whip.
6. Arrange some kiwi & strawberries along the sides of the wall.
7. Put a layer of whip again. Keep in the fridge.
8. At serving time, top with 3-4 thin, tall pieces of apple slices with the peel. Drizzle some crush on them. Serve.